Counterspy

Other Titles of Interest from Potomac Books

Sacred Secrets: How Soviet Intelligence Operations
Changed American History
by Jerrold and Leona Schecter

Soldiers, Spies, and the Rat Line:
America's Undeclared War Against the Soviets
by Col. James V. Milano, USA (Ret.) and Patrick Brogan

Stealing Secrets, Telling Lies: How Spies and Codebreakers
Helped Shape the Twentieth Century
by James Gannon

Counterspy

Memoirs of a Counterintelligence Officer in World War II and the Cold War

RICHARD W. CUTLER

Foreword by Joseph E. Persico

Potomac Books, Inc.
Washington, D.C.

Library of Congress Cataloging-in-Publication Data

Cutler, Richard W.
    Counterspy : memoirs of a counterintelligence office in World War II and the Cold War / Richard W. Cutler : foreword by Joseph E. Persico.— 1st ed.
      p. cm.
    Includes bibliographical references and index.
    ISBN 1-57488-839-0 (alk. paper)
    1. Cutler, Richard W.   2. United States. War Dept. Strategic Services Unit.
3. World War, 1939–1945—Secret Service—United States.   4. Intelligence service—United States—History—20th century.   5. World War, 1939–1945—Campaigns—Europe.   6. World War, 1939–1945—Personal narratives, American.
7. Intelligence officers—United States—Biography.   I. Title.

D810.S8C883   2004
940.54′8673′092—dc22   2004003587
ISBN 1-57488-846-3 (paperback)

Potomac Books, Inc.
22841 Quicksilver Drive
Dulles, Virginia 20166

First Edition

10 9 8 7 6 5 4 3 2 1

Contents

Foreword

YEARS AGO, I WAS LOOKING FOR AN UNTOLD STORY OF WORLD WAR II as a subject for my next book. My quest was answered when William Cunliffe, a sharp-eyed archivist at the National Archives, tipped me off to a history about to be declassified, revealing secret operations during the war conducted by America's first intelligence organization, the Office of Strategic Services (OSS). "Take a look at the German operations," Cunliffe advised me. It was for me exciting to discover that the OSS had penetrated Nazi Germany with more than two hundred spies. Subsequently, after tracking down dozens of people who had recruited, controlled, and documented these agents, as well as the spies themselves, I wrote *Piercing the Reich: The Penetration of Nazi Germany by American Secret Agents during World War II.* Over the course of the project, I immensely enjoyed interviewing the people who actually carried off this espionage triumph. Still, I was merely an observer, and whatever I would eventually write had to be second hand. No layman's account could substitute for being there. That is the irresistible appeal of Richard Cutler's *Counterspy.* Cutler was there, in the arena, an articulate, insightful, and reflective participant in operations from World War II into the dawning of the Cold War.

His end of the game was counterintelligence, which still remains the most mysterious and opaque to people outside that world. We generally know what secret agents do. They gather intelligence by whatever means their ingenuity may devise on the enemy's location, strength, armament, resources, and intentions in wartime, and in a tentative time of peace, such as the Cold War, on an adversary's internal politics, international aims, military secrets, and weapons developments. But what do counterspies do? Although I have written widely in the field, I never had so clear a picture of counterintelligence until reading Cutler's manuscript. He was indeed there, hands on, up to his elbows, fingernails not always clean (as this profession occasionally demands). His definition of the game is the shortest and most pointed of all I have come across, "tracking enemy agents and either neutralizing them or converting them into double agents who spied for the United States while pretending to spy for the enemy." In other words, spies fighting spies, or fighting fire with fire.

Cutler was a young man when he entered the game at twenty-seven. Yet his responsibilities, imposed by the demands of war, would tax a top executive in the most exacting peacetime occupation. For example, my book describes missions carried out by agents courageous or foolhardy enough to parachute into Nazi Germany to conduct espionage in a country held in the fearsome grip of the Gestapo. So far, so good. But how could the OSS know that these agents were bona fide and not double agents who could return to Germany carrying the secrets of how American espionage worked, or merely opportunists eager to pocket their OSS cash, or simply German POWs looking for a free trip home to the *Vaterland* at OSS expense? One of Cutler's first jobs was to "vet," that is ascertain the reliability of, these agents beforehand. His counterintelligence duties also involved him in a World War II supersecret that the rest of the world would not know about for another generation, Ultra. Cutler was among a handful of Americans allowed to use the product of this historic code-breaking enterprise through which British intelligence was reading the supposedly unbreakable German Enigma encryptions. By reading decrypted enemy messages, Cutler and his associates learned, in effect, from the Germans themselves who their agents were, where they operated, and what cover stories and code names they used; it was a counterintelligence bonanza.

With the war over and most Americans going home, Cutler stayed on and became an early recruit in the frontline trenches of the Cold War. His accounts of working within the tangled web of former German intelligence officials, the Soviet NKVD (Peoples' Commissariat for State Security), and the rival U.S. Army Counterintelligence Corps, among rascals, renegades, and the real thing, amidst the crazy quilt pattern of devastation and quasinormality in postwar Europe, reads like a LeCarré source book.

There is a bonus to Cutler's story that extends beyond espionage. He has a sharp eye and ear and sensitively recreates the feel of daily life in London amidst German V-weapon attacks; depicts how the Germans he encountered handled, rationalized, or ignored their war guilt; and describes the yawning gulf between clever, ruthless Soviet intelligence operatives and the appealing openness of Russian soldiers, the ordinary Ivan.

Cutler vividly conveys the contradictory emotions of the life he led. "No activity is more exciting and nerve-wracking," he says, "than spying," and he proves this on almost every page. He had become addicted, as if to a cerebral drug, driving himself so obsessively that he once collapsed from exhaustion and had to be sent away to recuperate. In the end, he had to choose between a promising career in the law, from which the war had detoured him (and which had begun in the law firm of William J. Dononvan, the very "Wild Bill" who subsequently created the OSS) or sticking with counterintelligence. He had just about chosen the latter when he received some practical advice from Donovan. Climbing the career ladder would be slow, slogging work during a period when a suspicious President Harry Truman was dismantling the OSS and when its surviving remnant, the Strategic Services Unit, was practically starving to death. Donovan advised Cutler to return to the law, make his career and possibly his bundle, and return some day to government at a high level. It was a formula that had worked for Donovan. And consider Cutler's OSS contemporary, William J. Casey, who left the organization at war's end, made a fortune in the law and business, and returned thirty years later to become the controversial director of Central Intelligence.

Cutler's career veered from espionage, but his interest and keen insight never did. Some of the most penetrating passages in this book deal with his analysis of why American intelligence failed before the disaster of September 11. We will save his sage conclusions for the reader. Cutler, however, pulls no punches in pinpointing the worst sin in the intelligence game, and that is when honest findings are twisted to fit political ends.

In the end, Cutler took the old spymaster Donovan's advice and went back to the law, where he indeed succeeded. Given his sure grasp of what continues to ail our intelligence—and counterintelligence—services, however, we almost wish he had stayed on.

I kept thinking of something else as I read this affecting manuscript. Eyewitness accounts such as Cutler's about World War II and the early Cold War belong to a fast vanishing breed. Thus, such firsthand reportage becomes all the more priceless.

Richard Cutler has pulled us into into a life, as he says, hooked on intelligence. And, frankly, I was hooked on his story.

Joseph E. Persico

Preface

SOME OF US WHO TOILED IN THE SHADOWS IN WORLD WAR II HAD exciting roles. Mine was counterespionage for the Office of Strategic Services (OSS), the forerunner of the Central Intelligence Agency (CIA). Our work required us to stay abreast of the war's progress, work that, being both a news junkie and history buff, I relished. My colleagues and I were tasked with tracking enemy agents and either neutralizing them or converting them into double agents who spied for the United States while pretending to spy for the enemy.

This is a memoir of my experiences in Britain, France, and especially Germany in the tumultuous mid-1940s. To reassemble the past I depended on my own recollections and those of surviving colleagues— the excitement of espionage burned certain facts into our memory—as well as personal letters and OSS documents retrieved from the National Archives. My memory was jogged by more than two hundred fact-filled letters home that described unclassified military and political events that I witnessed, such as Anthony Eden performing in Parliament and one of the Nuremberg war crimes trials. My family never discarded anything.

A few colleagues from those years were still living when I wrote this memoir. Before his death, Richard Helms, briefly my boss in Berlin and later director of the CIA, verified certain key details and provided other missing ones. Tom Polgar, my astute assistant in Berlin who later served at various times in high CIA positions—chief of mission for Germany, Vietnam, and Mexico—helped paint what we and our adversaries in Soviet intelligence did during the frenzied start of the Cold War. At the sixtieth anniversary of the founding of the OSS, held at CIA headquarters on June 7, 2002, OSS veterans and historians provided additional information.

A number of books, not least John Keegan's *Second World War,* proved invaluable in supplying facts about the raging war in which OSS played a small, yet crucial, role. In *Donovan and the CIA: A History of the Establishment of the CIA*, Thomas Troy documents how OSS chief Maj. Gen. William Donovan laid the foundation for the CIA and how Washington rivalries caused Truman to terminate OSS on October 1, 1945. And in *The Double Cross System in the War of 1939–45*, former British Security Service (MI-5) officer J. C. Masterson describes how British intelligence doubled all German agents in England and fed them misleading information to send back to Germany. A technical, but highly useful, book, *Fortitude: The D-Day Deception Campaign*, by MI-5 technician Roger Hesketh, presents the false reports of doubled German agents that fooled Hitler into believing the Normandy landing was a feint, a fatal mistake on his part.

In *The Gentleman Spy: The Life of Allen Dulles*, Peter Grose records how Dulles became the master American spy by uncovering German war secrets from anti-Nazi sources in or close to Hitler's government. Joseph Persico's *Piercing the Reich: The Penetration of Germany by American Secret Agents in World War II* traces how the OSS sent nearly two hundred agents into Germany. John H. Waller, an X-2 officer in London and Cairo, wrote a masterful account, *The Unseen War in Europe: Espionage and Conspiracy in the Second World War*. The best account of X-2's objectives and operations appears in Timothy Naftali's Harvard dissertation, "X-2 and the Apprenticeship of American Espionage, 1942–44," parts of which will appear in his forthcoming book *X-2: The Origins of American Counterespionage and Counterterrorism*. Tim helped me immensely by procuring OSS documents from the National Archives in Washington, corresponding frequently, and critiquing an early draft of this book during a long session in Honolulu.

It is my hope that this book will provide fresh insight into the world of counterespionage recreated by such worthy historians. My personal story reveals much about how counterespionage operations were planned and conducted in those pre-CIA days and why certain operations succeeded while others failed. Material that has not previously come to light, to my knowledge, includes the vetting or revetting of American agents from London because Donovan and the British government were not confident that OSS had run adequate background checks on new agents; how Lt. Gen. Lucius D. Clay, commander of American occupation forces in Berlin, naively assured Marshal Sokolovsky, his Soviet counterpart, that the United States would not spy on its Soviet allies while the Strategic Services Unit (SSU), OSS's successor, was doing just that, with Washington's

secret approval and without Clay's knowledge; how the CIA in Berlin recruited the head of the Soviet intelligence registry as an agent in place and for a whole year received copies of agents' messages to Moscow; and how SSU aborted a Soviet effort to kidnap a nuclear scientist after he refused Stalin's invitation to work on developing an atomic bomb.

When I started writing this book in July of 1992, I scarcely realized the scope of the task. Fortunately, the surprises arrived in digestible installments. The first roadblock came when a quick search of my basement produced just a slim batch of wartime letters home. After I had done much writing, four other batches emerged, over tantalizingly long intervals. My younger sister, Barlow Cutler Wotton, went to her attic and found some letters I wrote her during the war, as well as correspondence from Owen Keeling of Wimbledon, England, to my mother. My sister then encouraged our two nieces, Jean Nichols and Sandra Nichols Ward, to search their New Mexico and Massachussets homes, where they found, in mouse-nibbled shoe boxes, wartime letters I had written to my elder sister Janet Nichols. Several years later, while cleaning out obsolete files in my basement, I discovered the largest batch of letters yet—several hundred I had written to my mother between 1926 and 1946.

In researching, I wrote often to former colleagues in the air force and OSS, as well as to old friends. Many of these correspondents were helpful, including Ed Washburn, a former second lieutenant in the Air Force Combat Intelligence School at Harrisburg, Pennsylvania, who provided insights into the operations of America's most secret agency, the Special Branch of the War Department's Army Intelligence (G-2), which analyzed and disseminated intercepted enemy communications.

Seasoned CIA veteran Tom Polgar, my scholarly assistant in Berlin, reviewed countless drafts with patience, tact, and rare insight. He added facts, deleted errors, and vastly improved my descriptions of German and Soviet intelligence agencies and American operations against them. In addition to providing leads to historical sources, Tom gave me guidelines on what not to disclose and how to camouflage biographical facts about agents who put their lives on the line to serve the United States.

In 1946 my favorite spy in Berlin, Zig-Zag, took time between risky assignments to catalog hundreds of my European photos. Without his generous help, the graphics in this book would not have been possible.

Finally, extracting the essence of my espionage career at the end of World War II and the start of the Cold War—from memory, contemporary correspondence, official documents, and histories, enlivened by interviews with former colleagues and spies—and then fitting each part into its appropriate place in the mosaic, with incisive help from my gifted editor, Constance Buchanan, was one of the most enjoyable, absorbing, and useful tasks of my life.

Introduction

IN NOVEMBER 1945 GREAT GOOD LUCK PLACED ME IN BERLIN. I WAS all of twenty-eight years old and wore the uniform of first lieutenant in the U.S. Army Air Force, though my job had nothing to do with airplanes. Having left the top-secret B-29 Super-Fortress bomber program in Kansas fifteen months earlier, I was serving in Berlin as chief of counterespionage for the War Department's Strategic Services Unit (SSU). That obscure agency had just replaced America's first clandestine espionage service, the Office of Strategic Services (OSS). In turn, in 1947, SSU would be replaced by the Central Intelligence Agency (CIA).

No sooner had the Soviet Union battered Berlin into submission in May 1945 than it set about recruiting former German intelligence officers to spy on its wartime allies—specifically, on the American and British armies of occupation. My prime assignment was to uncover Soviet agents in Berlin, learn their objectives, and employ countermeasures. SSU collaborated with the U.S. Army's intelligence arm (G-2) and Counterintelligence Corps (CIC). Sometimes, on a hit-or-miss basis, G-2 handed me a dangerous lead, and I was thrust into the hidden world of Soviet espionage.

One day the colonel in charge of G-2 asked me to come right away to his office in the Telefunken building in the eastern part of the American-occupied sector of Berlin. When I got there, he reported that CIC had found a Soviet People's Commissariat for State Security (NKVD) lieutenant, apparently a drug addict, in a stupor on the sidewalk outside of a nightclub. (The NKVD was later renamed the Committee for State Security, or KGB.) CIC whisked the inebriated officer off to a hospital and put him in restraints to protect him from hurting himself. Then, he blurted out his wish to defect.

The G-2 colonel was visibly troubled as he told me the story. He didn't want to be accused by the Soviets of holding one of their men prisoner, but the man, if he truly was a defector, could prove to be a valuable source of information about Soviet intelligence. As the representative of America's new espionage agency, would I take this mixed-up Russian off G-2's hands? This wouldn't be any simple handoff. First, we would have to find a place where the defector could be detained without Soviet knowledge. The hospital was too public. Then, we would have to determine whether he could recover from his drug addiction and estimate how much he could disclose about Soviet intelligence operations in Berlin. I promptly got approval to relieve G-2 of its hot property from SSU-Germany headquarters in Wiesbaden and their superiors in Washington.

A much-relieved colonel discharged the Russian to me. After concocting a plausible identity for him—we told the hospital staff he was a German drug addict with a dangerous political past—we arranged to have "Vladimir," as we called him, confined temporarily in a treatment ward at the American hospital.

Admitting our charge to this hospital presented an unexpected challenge. The facility was located near the part of Berlin occupied by the Soviet Army, and Soviet troops frequently charged into the hospital in search of penicillin, waving machine guns at the terrified German staff until they got what they demanded. The soldiers had two reasons for wanting the antibiotics: to treat venereal diseases and to avoid the severe punishment the Soviets meted out to those who contracted these infections.[1]

Only the West Point colonel in charge of the hospital was to know Vladimir's true identity. In light of the sensitive situation, however, I wondered if he would allow our Russian to remain on the premises. It didn't help that we in SSU had been required to surrender our prestigious "Eisenhower passes" entitling the bearer, by order of the general, to enter any military area. They'd been taken away for a most sensible reason: Any SSU operative who fell into hostile hands with a pass would be unable to claim he was an ordinary soldier. So, I had no documentation to certify that I was part of the hush-hush secret service and bore responsibilities far higher than my military rank of first lieutenant would suggest. Time was short, and I decided not to beat around the bush.

"How do you do, Colonel? Did G-2 call to say I'd be coming in this morning?"

"Yes."

"Sir, I have an unusual request to make. I represent the Strategic Services Unit, successor to the Office of Strategic Services. Have you heard of it?"

"No."

"Well, SSU is America's new secret service, created by President Roosevelt and headquartered in the Pentagon under General Magruder. We conduct espionage and counterespionage. Right now we have a problem: The Soviet forces are using German intelligence officers to spy on us. We want to find out all we can about what they're seeking to learn and who they're using to do it.

"This week, G-2 Berlin came across a Soviet lieutenant who they think is a drug addict and who says he wishes to defect to American intelligence. He's here in the contagious diseases ward. We'd like him to be kept here. G-2, through the provost mall's office, will provide guards. While the doctors determine the extent of his addiction and give treatment, we'll start interrogation to learn whether he is the real article or just a plant the Russkies put there to fool us."

The colonel responded quickly, "Lieutenant, armed Soviet troops come in here after penicillin from time to time. It's too risky. You'll have to get this Russian out of here."

"Sir," I argued, seeing a prized opportunity slipping away, "espionage operations always involve danger. I realize you don't know me and I'm only a first lieutenant—the SSU is secret; we don't carry Eisenhower passes—but I assure you what I'm doing has been approved by the highest authority. And there's a way you can verify my bona fides—you can call General Sibert in Frankfurt, the G-2 for the European theater."

This was part bluff. Sibert, to my knowledge, hadn't heard of this particular operation, though he was familiar with SSU-Berlin and its frontline position in the escalating espionage game. He might back me up. Fortunately, the colonel agreed without making the call, urging me to get the soldier out of his hospital as soon as possible.

Vladimir gave us enough biographical data that we could check the truthfulness of at least part of his story. Claiming his father had been in the diplomatic service in Stockholm and Copenhagen, he listed specific street addresses in cities where they had lived and explained he'd learned his good German at home because his father had used it in his profession. He identified the location of his NKVD office in Berlin, temptingly adding that it had a network of spies specifically aimed at learning secrets about the Americans. I immediately cabled Washington to verify the addresses in Stockholm and Copenhagen where the defector claimed to have lived. While that check was being completed, the doctors said that Vladimir's addiction could be kept in check so long as he was hospitalized. Washington responded with a troubling report. The streets in Stockholm and Copenhagen did exist, but there was no residence at one address and, for some reason I no longer recall, Vladimir couldn't have lived at the other address.

Obviously, our patient wasn't being fully honest. He might be a German imposter posing as a Russian, we thought, or a Russian plant who wished to become a double agent against the United States. We nearly abandoned his case. On the slim chance that he was a true defector, we didn't, for until then the United States had not had the benefit of a single Soviet intelligence defector. I decided to have Vladimir interrogated by a Russian-born American officer who could ascertain his true nationality. The interrogator was a translator who worked for top American officers at meetings with their Soviet counterparts at the Berlin *Kommandatura*, the joint office of the four occupying powers, Soviet, American, British, and French.[2]

The translator's analysis clinched the case.

"Lieutenant, he's clearly a Russian. He speaks Russian with a distinct peasant accent. However, his German is flawless. His vocabulary approaches the German poet Heine's. I know the type. There's a Russian saying that goes, 'In every dung heap there is one piece of gold.' No doubt he was a very bright peasant student from the provinces who was picked for advanced education in Moscow and learned his proper German there."

The defector's fluent German explained why he would have been recruited for Soviet espionage, and he did seem to know something about the NKVD. While we were puzzling over the intelligence value of a drug addict, a report came in that shook the intelligence community. According to CIC, "two thousand Soviet troops" were combing Berlin for Vladimir. CIC based this seemingly wild estimate on the fact that several large NKVD squads were storming in and out of Russian haunts all over the city. That search could be a Russian effort to give credibility to the man's claim to be a defector when in fact he was their plant. More likely, it could mean they were frantic to find him because he might spill valuable information. The Soviets were paranoid about maintaining secrecy.

On the chance that Vladimir could yield useful information about Soviet intelligence personnel, objectives, and methods of operation, SSU headquarters in Washington authorized me to move Vladimir out of Berlin to lessen the chance of confrontation between Soviet troops and his captors. I was to fly him from Tempelhof Airfield in downtown Berlin to Frankfurt-am-Main, in the American zone of occupied Germany. There, Russian-speaking interrogators would debrief Vladimir, and doctors would treat his addiction. The colonel at the hospital was relieved.

Soon after the conquering Allies agreed to share the occupation of Germany by dividing the country into four zones and Berlin into four sectors—for Soviet, American, British, and French armies—the Soviets sought to undermine their allies' ability to govern their respective sectors of Berlin. Therefore, it was unsafe to try to keep Vladimir there, and moving him would be tricky. We dressed him in a U.S. Army uniform, and I drove him to Tempelhof. In early November Berlin, like London, can be buried in dense fogs, and this day was a classic example. A heavy one rolled in and abruptly closed the airport. I returned my captive to the hospital for the night, much to the colonel's displeasure. The fog lingered, and the next day the colonel, agitated over the prospect of detection, ordered me to remove Vladimir from the hospital for good.

I went to G-2. They arranged to reopen a detention camp that had once held German prisoners. I put Vladimir in the hands of an armed guard and had him dress in civilian clothing, taking away his belt in case he was suicidal. Then, we waited, twiddling our thumbs until the airport resumed operations. I had been up until the wee hours for several nights running and was getting little sleep. Meanwhile, SSU was getting jittery over the delay.

Earlier in my OSS career, during training outside Washington, I'd been taught that when you wish to conceal your move from the enemy, think of what they would least expect you to do. The Soviets would speculate that if we attempted to take Vladimir out of Berlin, we would transport him by air since they couldn't control American flights. But would they think us so foolish as to drive Vladimir through the Russian zone, 110 miles down the autobahn to Helmstedt, at the eastern tip of the British zone? No. They would never think we'd be that brash. So that was my answer.

I told the motor pool to prepare my car for a long trip—I was going to Switzerland. Once again we had Vladimir dress in an American uniform. I told him in German that if he cooperated, he could have a villa in Chicago. That was sheer bluff, but he acted as if he believed me. There remained the question of how to get through the Soviet Army checkpoint as we left Berlin to enter the Russian zone, and then again through a second Soviet checkpoint when we left it to enter the British zone.

There were many risks. Although there was a treaty guaranteeing American military access to the autobahn connecting Berlin with the British zone, the Russian border guards might inspect our car. Of greater concern, Vladimir, if he became squeamish about defecting, or had been a plant all along, might cry out that he was a captured prisoner. Moreover, if we did manage to slip past the guards, we might easily become lost on the poorly marked autobahn with its elaborate clover leaves that ringed Berlin. We knew of Americans who had missed the turn at night and been arrested by the Russians for straying off the approved autobahn and entering the forbidden Soviet zone.

I reasoned that the Russians either feared or were in awe of high rank, notwithstanding all their talk about being a classless society. So on November 9, the day we departed for Frankfurt, I attached a lieutenant colonel's insignia to my uniform for the trip. Then, I put a pack of rare Camel cigarettes on the dashboard to give the Soviet border guards as a token of friendship. We had radically Americanized Vladimir. Besides his new American uniform, he now had chewing gum and a crew cut. If he helped us, I told him again, he could have that villa in Chicago. If not, two burly SSU sergeants seated on either side of him would take matters into their own hands. Each was armed with a .45 caliber semiautomatic pistol and had instructions to nudge them into Vladimir's ribs as we approached the Soviet checkpoints.

When we came in sight of the checkpoint while exiting Berlin, I turned the radio on to a station playing American jazz. My heart was pounding so loudly, I could almost hear it over the music. At any minute I could be on my way to a Soviet prison for some rough interrogation. Although Washington had approved my transporting this defector out of Berlin, one key figure had not been informed—Lt. Gen. Lucius D. Clay, the deputy military governor for the American occupation forces, who was stationed in Berlin. Unfortunately, Clay had voluntarily assured Marshal Sokolosky, his Soviet counterpart, that the United States would not engage in espionage against them. Reportedly, he thought the Soviets were overly suspicious about American espionage and disbelieved reports that the Soviets were already spying on Americans. That presented a dilemma for SSU-Washington, which decided to continue spying and not inform Clay, presumably with War Department approval, no doubt feeling that the naïvité of a general should not block its mission to protect

America from rampant espionage by a new, hostile, heavily armed force. If I ended up in a Soviet jug, General Clay could make it very hot for me, unless Washington forcefully intervened. Would they?

My mind darted back to the good old days of comparative safety when I had served with the B-29 program in Kansas. Was my transfer into espionage such a wise one?

We had been on the road only a short time when I drove up to the large red and green pole blocking our entrance to the Soviet zone. Two grim-looking Russian guards ambled out of their guardhouse into the frigid November air, machine guns slung from their shoulders.

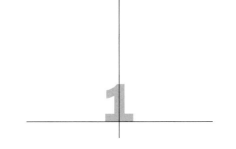

A BIG SURPRISE

IN MID-JULY 1944, FIFTEEN MONTHS BEFORE VLADIMIR AND I SET out for Frankfurt-am-Main, I was an Army Air Forces second lieutenant training B-29 flight crews. We were part of the 500th Very-Heavy Bomb Group stationed at Walker, Kansas, amid endless fields of wheat. Even as American and British troops were breaking out from the Normandy beaches into France, the United States was feverishly preparing to bomb Tokyo from islands in the mid-Pacific. The B-29 bombers had been specially designed to travel 1,500 miles from these islands to Japan and return. The Marines were about to capture Guam, Tinian, and Saipan as bases from which to attack Japan.

As one of thirteen combat intelligence officers, I taught pilots, navigators, flight engineers, gunners, and bombardiers how to distinguish between friendly and Japanese airplanes, what tactics the Japanese Air Force used, how to identify targets from various altitudes, and how to ditch into the Pacific and survive while awaiting air-sea rescue. Later, in combat we would brief flight crews on mission targets and help them identify checkpoints along the way. We would also debrief them on the success of their bombing runs.

Two assignments in Kansas were particularly enjoyable. I gave news lectures on the war's progress worldwide and published a two-page daily news bulletin for our bomb group personnel. The army provided no reliable war news. To fill the void, I copied two-day-old *New York Times* war maps on stencil paper, adding current enemy and Allied battle lines as reported in the Kansas City morning newspaper and on radio. Different colors highlighted the German and Allied battle lines in Normandy. Airmen repeatedly asked me what my "secret sources" were. Nowhere in the army had they seen such maps.

By mid-July 1944, after a stint as special assistant to the chief of the trade intelligence division of the Board of Economic Warfare in Washington, followed by eighteen months of intensive military training, I was looking forward to going off to war. I was thrilled to hear from our resourceful adjutant, Major Lloyd, that when the 500th Bomb Group went overseas, we would acquire our own radio transmitter capable of broadcasting a distance of fifty miles. The bomb group wanted me to broadcast war news twice a day to an audience much larger than our unit. The major didn't mention a probable contributing cause of this future assignment: higher echelons, the Seventy-Third Wing and Twentieth Bomber Command, had requested that I be transferred to them to give daily news broadcasts.

A week later my commanding officer, Col. Richard T. King Jr., West Point '35, summoned me to his office. I was concerned because shortly after meeting him, I had committed a major faux pas. I had mentioned that when I was a boy of thirteen I'd attended an Army-Yale football game with my father. "Sir," I asked, "do you know the member of that Army football team who tackled a Yale player so hard he died on the field?"

The colonel replied: "I made the tackle."

I need not have worried over the summons. The colonel spoke quickly. "Lieutenant, we're going to ship out soon. The group will fly to Guam as soon as the Marines drive out the Japs. Then we'll bomb Tokyo from there. You're to travel with the ground troops to Los Angeles. They'll be bored stiff traveling five days by train. En route I want you to put out a daily newspaper on the war. In Los Angeles they may have to wait three weeks for transport to Guam, serving as stevedores in the interim. No one can predict when the Marines will secure our bases. The soldiers won't like stevedoring and waiting. You're to continue the newspaper and give news briefs on the status of the war and why we are fighting. That'll help morale, just as your talks have done on this base.

"And Lieutenant, one other thing—we're going to build a transmitter on Guam to broadcast to ships and planes throughout the central Pacific. I want you, as extra duty, to give daily broadcasts on how the war is going. You can take a week's emergency pre-overseas furlough and report back by next Tuesday."

Major Lloyd had not been blowing smoke in predicting my role.

I pointed out to Colonel King that I couldn't have written his base's daily news bulletin without the help of the *New York Times*. Could I ask the army for permission to receive, uncensored, both the *Times* and transcripts of the daily radio broadcasts by commentator Raymond Graham Swing? I explained that I knew and had corresponded with Swing. I could ask permission in person by stopping at the Pentagon on my way home to see my parents in Connecticut. The colonel agreed, and soon thereafter I went to the recently built Pentagon.

Washington joked about the Pentagon's being the world's largest office building. They spoke of people venturing into it and not coming out for days. I was walking through the maze of corridors, trying to find my way to the appropriate office, when a familiar face emerged from scores of officers busily scurrying by. He was the red-haired major who had interviewed me at the Army Air Forces Combat Intelligence School in Pennsylvania and expressed an interest in my joining the Office of Strategic Services (OSS), the new U.S. intelligence agency. I still hadn't heard any official follow-up. Twice I had tried to get into OSS and been turned down.

"Lieutenant," he said, hailing me, "aren't you the one I interviewed for OSS at Harrisburg?"

"Yes, Major."

"What brings you to the Pentagon?" No sooner had I explained than he replied, "You're coming with us."

"But Major, that can't be. I'm on tactical alert for immediate overseas shipment by my army air force unit. Regulations forbid the transfer of personnel out of such units."

"Go to Q Street in Georgetown, and you'll see," he said, handing me a card with the address. After getting the sought-after permission from the Pentagon, I went to the Q Street office, but it was after hours, and the place was closed. I quickly dismissed the major's comments. He must have been referring to some OSS request that the army air force transfer me to OSS, I thought. The air force would have noted my unit's overseas alert status and turned it down. Clearly, the major's information must be dated.

I proceeded to Westport to see my parents. My father made a special trip home from Patterson, New Jersey, where he held a wartime job at a Curtiss-Wright factory that was cranking out B-29 engines. He enjoyed telling workmen at the rapidly expanding factory that his son was with the B-29s and using *their* engines, an expression of fatherly pride that was to become surprisingly significant later.

During my brief furlough a telegram arrived from Colonel King's adjutant: "Departure date moved up to Saturday from Tuesday. Report to Floyd Bennett Air Field in NYC tomorrow to take plane back to Walker."

At the field I found a B-17 Flying Fortress waiting for me, the sole passenger. The flight crew came from my B-29 unit. They too were going overseas shortly after a last fling in New York. How much they had enjoyed themselves, I would soon find out. I chatted with them briefly as we flew over the Statue of Liberty heading west, then went back to my seat. With nothing to do, I decided to measure our course by studying the ground and the maps. Suddenly, it occurred to me that we were headed not westerly toward Kansas, but northwesterly toward Toronto or Detroit. I dashed into the cockpit to alert the pilot. He had set the plane on automatic pilot and was fast asleep along with his co-pilot and navigator. That must have been a wild fling they had, I concluded, shaking them awake.

On arrival at Walker Air Base, learning that the troop train was fully loaded with ground crews and awaiting my arrival, I scrambled to the bachelor officers quarters (BOQ) to pick up my gear. The phone rang. It was Saturday night, and no one else was in the BOQ. Thinking that some pilot's family or sweetheart was trying to reach him, I picked up the phone and got a big surprise.

"Get your ass over to my office!" Major Lloyd barked. "The colonel is madder'n hell."

"But Major, I'm on overseas alert and the train is waiting."

"A telegram came from Washington today ordering you to report for duty there. Colonel King figures you used your time in Washington to avoid overseas duty with us, that you chickened out to avoid the fighting."

I was thunderstruck. The charge was monstrously false. I raced to the adjutant's office where he showed me the telegram. Lieutenant General Ulio, adjutant general of the U.S. Army, had ordered me to report to him in the Pentagon within forty-eight hours for reassignment. "This order has to be a mistake," I blurted out. It violated an ironclad army rule banning personnel transfers out of units on tactical alert for overseas shipment. Without this rule a unit could go into battle understaffed. I added that I wanted to go to Saipan with the 500th both because I was very much attached to it and to refute the colonel's slur that I had connived to shirk combat duty. Thinking more like an attorney—which I had been before the war—than a lowly second lieutenant, I suggested to Major Lloyd that he advise Colonel King to call his immediate superior, the general in charge of the Seventy-Third Wing and explain why there must be an error.

Colonel King telephoned Colorado Springs and drew Brig. Gen. Rosie O'Donnell off the dance floor at the Broadmoor Hotel. King explained that I was one of his thirteen combat intelligence officers, especially useful because my newscasts to the troops had a favorable impact on their morale, and that Ulio's order mistakenly overlooked the tactical alert rule. O'Donnell, whose shoulders then carried one star, abruptly asked, "Who did you say signed that order?"

"General Ulio."

"Three stars!" He hung up.

That ended King's effort to keep me with the 500th Bomb Group. The next day, as a farewell, one of the pilots took me up in a small trainer plane and flew loop-the-loops to make me airsick—a practical joke, I figured. The pilots were impressed that I had been summoned to Washington by a lieutenant general and were as puzzled as I as to the reason.

Colonel King had been right—there was a delay of a month before the Marines conquered Saipan, Tinian, and Guam—and it wasn't until November 24 that B-29s started attacking Tokyo from Saipan and Tinian.

The scale of the bombing effort was enormous. On March 9, 1945, alone, 276 B-29s dropped some two thousand tons of incendiary bombs on Tokyo, destroying 40 percent of that city and killing more people[1] than either of the subsequent atomic bomb attacks on Hiroshima and Nagasaki. All told, American bombings inflicted more damage on Japan in six months than the Allies subjected Germany to in the last three years of the war.[2]

During the bombings, the barracks where I would have slept in Saipan burned down. A damaged B-29 returning from Tokyo crashed into it, killing several of my fellow officers. Would I have been one of them had my assignment not been changed? As for Colonel King, he was shot down over Japan in 1944, lost one hundred pounds in prison camp, survived the war, and became a general before retiring.

Of course, I knew none of this in early August 1944 when I set out for my undefined assignment in Washington. All I knew was that in the army, you had to expect the unexpected.

WELCOME TO OSS

WALKING DOWN THE LONG PENTAGON CORRIDOR TOWARD LIEU-tenant General Ulio's office, I was as uneasy as the Cowardly Lion approaching the great Oz. Why had the general in charge of all personnel policy summoned me to appear before him? The answer came quickly: An assistant handed over a new order transferring me from the U.S. Army Air Force to the ever-so-secret OSS.

At Q Street, OSS warmly welcomed me as a new member and promptly dissolved the mystery of what I was to do in OSS. I would be assigned to X-2, the counterespionage branch, and go to France after one or two months of training in Washington. Then I would fly to Algiers and serve with a special counterintelligence (SCI) unit. We would work with the French underground, or *Maquis,* as it was sometimes called, searching for any German agents left behind by Hitler's army as it retreated after the U.S.-planned invasion of southern France.

OSS also clarified how it had plucked me out of the army air force when I was en route to the Pacific. Gen. Hap Arnold, commanding officer of the air force, had complained at a meeting of the Joint Chiefs to OSS chief Maj. Gen. William J. "Wild Bill" Donovan, that OSS had not yet detected the location of German jet aircraft factories. They were rumored to be on the verge of production. Arnold stirred up a storm, forecasting that the superior speed of German jets would put the Allies, with their much-slower, conventional, prop-driven aircraft, at a disastrous disadvantage.

It just so happened that Donovan was a founding partner in a New York law firm—Donovan, Leisure, Newton, and Lumbard—for which I had briefly worked before the war. At the next meeting of the Joint Chiefs, Donovan was ready. He was a gifted lawyer who carefully marshaled persuasive facts.

"Have you discovered the location of the German jet airplane factories yet?" General Arnold asked.

"Look, Hap," Donovan replied, "it takes time to build OSS up to the size where we can cover all the assignments being thrown at us. It isn't easy getting the type of personnel we need. Right now, your air force has refused our request to release eleven lieutenants. We need them for their European language skills. You're sending them to the Pacific where those languages can be of no earthly use. Releasing them to us will help us get your data."

And so the Joint Chiefs waived the rule against transfers out of tactically alert units. After trying twice and failing to get into OSS, I felt blessed by the sheer dumb luck of having top generals and admirals shift my career in the hoped-for direction.

My euphoria soon wore off as I plunged, along with OSS's other new staff, into intensive indoctrination on espionage. OSS, we were told, was America's first secret service. President Franklin Delano Roosevelt had created it in June 1942 to provide many services not offered by the army's intelligence arm, G-2, and the Office of Naval Intelligence (ONI), which concentrated on analyzing the enemy's weapons, tactics, and force dispositions. Roosevelt wanted the ability to learn the enemy's plans through clandestine espionage. From the outset OSS operations were exclusively international, as opposed to Federal Bureau of Investigation (FBI) work, which was then limited to the Western Hemisphere, primarily the United States.

OSS chief Bill Donovan was a charming, audacious public figure who had heroically led New York's "Fighting" Sixty-Ninth Regiment in a bloody battle in World War I, an episode later memorialized in a movie. His subsequent distinguished civilian career included service as deputy attorney general of the United States under President Hoover. He had founded his own law firm at 2 Wall Street and was on a leave of absence during my short stint there from 1941 to 1942. I had met him twice at law firm parties, to which he returned from Washington like a conquering hero. A great appellate lawyer, he had argued five cases in front of the United States Supreme Court before the age of fifty.

President Roosevelt apparently admired Donovan. Or at least, with his customary shrewdness, he saw the political advantage of putting OSS in the hands of an Irish-American who was Republican, pro-British, and not an isolationist. Donovan was the political antithesis of Joseph E. Kennedy, the U.S. ambassador to Great Britain who frequently embarrassed Roosevelt by uttering isolationist and anti-British comments to the press.

In 1940 when France collapsed, Frank Knox, the Republican secretary of the navy, recommended to Roosevelt that he send Donovan to Europe to assess British morale and military capabilities. Donovan could also examine British intelligence and counterintelligence methods. Roosevelt agreed. Donovan, upon his return, reported favorably on Great Britain's military strength and will to fight on. He also recommended the creation of a clandestine U.S. intelligence service.

On July 15, 1941, Roosevelt created a new war intelligence agency that would report directly to *him*.[1] It bore an innocent-sounding name, the Office of Coordinator of Information, which was changed to the Office of Strategic Services after the United States entered the war. Roosevelt chose the resourceful Donovan as its head, stating that he had imagination and daring that traditional military officers lacked. OSS's functions ultimately included "an array of unconventional missions essential to modern war: espionage, counterespionage, deception, black propaganda, behind-the-lines guerrilla warfare, partisan liaison, covert political action, sabotage, maritime operations, and related technical support tasks."[2] FDR's choice of Donovan proved to be a wise one. Donovan loved people. His magnetic personality and boundless social energy enabled him to make and retain countless friends in high places. Roosevelt gave him carte blanche in recruiting for OSS, which Donovan took full advantage of.[3] According to Donovan's biographer, he "turned first to men whom he knew and trusted—bankers, lawyers, industrialists, and conservative academics. In their turn they recruited among those whom they knew and trusted; and this gave the Donovan agency its tinge of well-to-do Ivy League, often Republican, socially prominent men and women."[4]

OSS also included well-known civic leaders: David Bruce of the Mellon family, an Armour from Chicago, a Whitney from New York, Russell Forgan from the Glore Forgan investment banking firm, Allen Dulles of Sullivan and Cromwell in New York, James Baxter, the president of Williams College, and William Langer, a distinguished history professor at Harvard. Some retained civilian status, like Allen Dulles in Berne, Switzerland; others became naval captains or army colonels. OSS personnel serving in Washington were predominantly researchers and mostly civilian, while overseas they tended to be military.

Generally, OSS civilians were women and men too old for the draft. At the lower levels where I operated, most OSS staff were graduates of Ivy

League and Seven Sisters colleges. Recruits were often selected by former professors already inside OSS for their proficiency in foreign languages and familiarity with foreign lands. Little wonder that the widely syndicated gossip columnist Drew Pearson dubbed OSS "O So Social" and mocked it in his articles attacking the social establishment. "OSS is one of the fanciest groups of dilettante diplomats, Wall Street bankers, and amateur detectives ever seen in Washington,"[5] he sneered. Fifty-two years later, a better informed description concluded that Donovan's greatest contribution to the war came when he "quickly found, screened, trained, deployed, and above all, inspired" the diverse talent required to carry out OSS's many missions.[6]

I found my fellow OSS recruits highly educated, well traveled, and usually conversant in one or more foreign languages—in short, well suited to international intelligence work. The training also impressed me. In a weeklong intensive "camp" in Virginia, OSS subjected us to psychological tests to evaluate leadership skills, especially in dangerous unprecedented situations, like suddenly being in a lifeboat with strangers. The testers noted who took charge in the fictitious lifeboat and how they led the others. Instructors schooled us in deception, cover roles, confidentiality, and the use of espionage and bureaucratic lingo. We were also taught how to pick locks. The ease with which some of us mastered this skill demonstrated why we should never rely on locks to protect secret documents. Numbered among our teachers, so it was rumored, were experienced lock pickers released from prison for this overriding war effort.

OSS provided me with an excellent private tutor so that I could brush up on my French and reliably communicate with the French Resistance. I had last spoken and heard French nine years earlier in a French literature course at Yale. Anticipating that my future effectiveness and safety might depend on fluency, I progressed rapidly. I also practiced Spanish, which I had learned and spoken during a four-month trip through Latin America three years earlier.

By August I was anxious to be off, not least because the rapid progress of Allied armies through France might obliterate the need for my service. In late July OSS had explained that I would travel either to Algiers or to Caserta, near Naples, then be flown into southern France just behind the advancing U.S. Army. There I would be part of a special counterintelligence team of three: myself, a radio operator, and a member of the French Resistance. With the help of radio broadcasts from OSS-London, we would identify, describe, and locate German spies in France and ask the

French Resistance to trail them long enough to discover their associates. Then we would seek either to convert them into double agents, encourage the Resistance to "neutralize" them by making them social outcasts, or kill them. To kill too many agents run by any given German intelligence (*Abwehr*) officer would signal to him that his organization had a leak, thereby inducing him to change agents or switch tactics. Of course, we would also try to learn what information the German spies were after. Being young and adventurous, I had a taste for this sort of work, and I could hardly wait to get going.

The Seventh U.S. Army landed in southern France on August 15 and rapidly advanced north toward Patton's Third Army as it bolted from the Normandy beaches south and then east. The two armies linked up at Dijon on September 12, 1944, and things were swimming along until they ran out of scarce gasoline toward the end of the month. The Allies slowed down and the Germans dug in at the French border, protected by their fortified Siegfried Line.

While waiting for orders to go overseas, I took full advantage of the Washington scene. The nation's capital was buzzing with people working for the war effort, particularly, and luckily for me, females. The higher brass at the Pentagon, fearing congressional sensitivity to public opinion, had forbidden any officers below the rank of major to serve in that "cushy soft" spot and stationed captains and lieutenants miles away in Maryland.

Therefore as a second lieutenant I was a rarity in Washington. The military took pains to instruct me, "If anyone asks you what a second lieutenant is doing in Washington, say, 'I'm preparing for immediate overseas shipment.'" Dating was a breeze. I went dancing many a night, often accompanied by Roy Steyer, my shy Yale Law School classmate. After many months socially marooned with soldiers and wheat in Kansas, female companionship was most welcome.

In mid-September came another surprise: I would be heading to London, not Algiers or Caserta. One of my superiors at X-2 told me, "You're to go to London on the way to the Mediterranean. There you'll receive advanced training before proceeding to your ultimate takeoff point. You'll be assigned to the Mediterranean theater, but on detached service to London." Detached service carried a special supplementary allowance of seven dollars a day, a princely sum considering the army also paid for lodging, food, transportation, and incidentals such as medical care.

While awaiting orders, I visited my parents in Westport, Connecticut, and my sister Betty in New York. Betty worked for a naval architect and was engaged to marry Joe Matthews, a Marine lieutenant about to be shipped to the Pacific. Joe would be riddled with .22 caliber machine gun bullets at Okinawa, the bloodiest Pacific land battle, but would survive to complete his Yale education. My father was sorely disappointed that I had left the B-29s. He could imagine no war assignment of equal importance, and I could not tell him what I was about to do.

Finally, the travel orders came. A small detachment of Europe-bound OSSers traveled by train to New York. In the early morning we rumbled in army trucks through sleepy Manhattan streets and boarded the Cunard Line's requisitioned 45,650-ton SS *Acquitania*, along with several thousand troops. At long last, I was on my way to war.

3

ENIGMA, ULTRA, AND
DOUBLE CROSS

We boarded the four-stack SS *Acquitania* in the dark pre-dawn at her Hudson River pier. Thousands of troops solemnly shuffled up the gangplank and disappeared into the bowels of the ship. Stacked like sardines in bunks reaching from deck to ceiling, we joked about our cramped quarters and, less often, about German submarines. We had scarcely left New York Harbor when the captain announced that the *Acquitania* was so fast that she wouldn't need a destroyer escort. What he didn't say was that the *Acquitania*—the Cunard's second largest liner after the more famous *Queen Mary*—was the slowest ship not required to travel with a protective escort.

Everyone on board soon tired of shipboard routine—standing in long lines for mess, sitting in airless bunks, and occasionally walking on deck. To relieve the ennui I volunteered to broadcast war news over the ship's loudspeaker. The captain welcomed anything that might break the boredom.

After docking at Grenock, near Glasgow, the OSS contingent boarded a train for London. The Red Cross fed us doughnuts and hot coffee at train stops. The three-day journey seemed to last forever, with the train coming to a stop whenever air raid sirens screeched. Finally, London's red-brick skyline loomed ahead as dawn broke. Our train rolled ever more slowly toward its final stop in Euston station. As I stumbled onto the platform, groggy from lack of sleep, a well-dressed gentleman approached and barked out in a crisp English accent, "Are you the honorable *Leften*-ant Cutler?"

I could have died. The OSS group was supposed to be traveling secretly. The Englishman was Owen Keeling of Wimbledon, a family friend who had lent my father funds to build his first home after all of his savings had been lost in a Canadian bank failure.

"Can you come and stay with me in Wimbledon, old boy?"

"I have to report to my headquarters. Give me your phone number, and I'll call you after I find out."

Bone tired, our small detachment arrived at OSS headquarters on Grosvenor Square near the American embassy. We received British ration cards, instructions on housing, and identification cards enabling us to eat at the massive mess hall in the Grosvenor Hotel. It fed six thousand military mouths each day, cafeteria style. GIs aptly dubbed it Willow Run after the giant factory Henry Ford had built at Willow Run, Michigan, to crank out B-24 Liberator bombers, one every hour.

Our next stop was OSS counterespionage headquarters, or X-2, at 14 Ryder Street, just off Picadilly, the major east-west street linking Hyde Park and Picadilly Circus. Fourteen Ryder Street was a shabby, grotesque Victorian layer-cake building. The roof had been crudely rebuilt after being set afire by German bombs during the Blitz. Ryder Street also housed part of Section V, the counterespionage section of the British Intelligence Service (MI-6), Britain's international secret service. MI-6 had acquired its name long before, when it operated as military intelligence, but now it reported to the British Foreign Office. We walked through open offices on the ground floor where female military personnel in cubbyholes toiled over ancient typewriters, rode the squeaky elevator up to the top floor—reserved, we joked, for Americans because it was closest to the air raids—and were ushered into the offices of Norman Holmes Pearson, chief of X-2 Europe, for the official welcome. He was the epitome of a counterespionage chief—a cigarette-smoking, slightly hunch-backed Yale English instructor on leave, who relished clandestine hokeypokey and analyzing enemy tactics.

Along the run-down corridors on two floors American X-2 personnel worked closely with counterparts in MI-6's Section V, many of them Oxford and Cambridge graduates. Primarily, our enemy consisted of the two German foreign intelligence services: the traditional, elite *Abwehr* and the newer, Nazi-created *Sicherheitsdienst,* or Security Service. Ryder Street also provided offices for the few French, Belgian, and Dutch intelligence officers who communicated with resistance and intelligence networks in their occupied homelands. All Allied intelligence services recruited linguists, usually from the top universities, and no matter how drab the surroundings, there was a definite, elite air about the place. I shared offices with X-2 officers in training for duty in France. Quickly, X-2 disclosed the mysterious reason our group had been brought to London rather than the intended jumping-off point at Algiers or Caserta: Only in London, we were told, could the war's top secret be explained to us, and then only by its owner, the British.

Rapid indoctrination followed over the next few days. The MI-6 building's function was top secret. If a friend encountered me on the street and asked where I was going, or wanted to walk with me, I was to give him the slip, proceeding to Grosvenor Square and disappearing into a building innocuously known as an American military building.

We in X-2 received from our MI-6 counterparts the fruit of the greatest intelligence coup of World War II: the German military and diplomatic codes that Britain had painstakingly broken.[1] Before the war, most codes could be broken by clever, persistent cryptanalysts. Once a code was broken, subsequent messages could be deciphered quickly unless the sender altered the code. Most senders were trained to do that from time to time. Believing they could avoid the bother of changing codes by devising an unbreakable one, the German military, or *Wehrmacht*, had acquired what was thought to be the perfect code, theoretically incapable of being deciphered by even the most skilled cryptanalyists. The concept was deceptively simple: a cipher machine, named "Enigma" by the Germans, would electrically encipher or encode each message in such a way that it could be deciphered only by a similar machine at the receiver's end.

In 1939 Polish intelligence gained temporary possession of a German Enigma machine in a Warsaw railroad station, photographed it extensively, and built a replica, which they gave to the British Secret Service in Paris. The French counterespionage service gave the British the instructions and keys to Enigma. Back in England at Bletchley Park, which housed Britain's code-breaking agency, the British spent months tinkering with the machine until they were able to get it to work. Subsequently, they obtained a second machine in perfect working order from a German submarine that had been forced to surface in the Atlantic.

In late 1941 a cryptanalyst named Dillwyn Knox broke the Enigma code, and for the next four years the British received, decoded, and translated top-secret German diplomatic, military, and naval communications without German knowledge. The intercepts were called ISK, for Intelligence Service Knox.[2]

The Germans put only top-secret messages on Enigma and sent them only between stations where the machine, as bulky as a big typewriter, could be placed. A hand-cipher code was deemed sufficiently secure for other German secrets. In 1940 the British also broke this code; these intercepts were labeled ISOS, for Intelligence Service Oliver Strachey, the code breaker.[3]

All intercepts, whether ISK or ISOS, were classified as "Ultra." Throughout the war, Ultra was kept secret by closely restricting the need to know. The few who did know included Donovan, a handful of his top aides in Washington, and members of X-2, all of whom first received individual security clearance by British intelligence. The Brits, we were told, routinely rejected Americans of German ethnic background. The key to British success in preserving their secret was never to utilize intercepted messages in a way that might arouse German suspicion about codes being broken. According to one oft-repeated, apocryphal tale, Winston Churchill learned through Enigma that the German *Luftwaffe* was going to annihilate Coventry as it had Rotterdam in 1940. Churchill, it is said, declined to order Royal Air Force (RAF) fighters to intercept the incoming *Luftwaffe* bombers lest the Germans suspect that the British had been forewarned.

Again and again, our British indoctrinators preached that protecting the secret required sacrificing some targets to the enemy. They emphasized to us that the U.S. Army Air Force under American Navy command had been extremely foolish to shoot down Japanese admiral Isoroku Yamamoto in the South Pacific after the U.S. Navy broke the Japanese naval code. Thanks to that intelligence coup, the Americans had already won the decisive Battle of Midway in June 1942. In April 1943, Yamamoto, leader of the attack on Pearl Harbor, was scheduled to fly from Rabaul to Ballale, a forward Japanese position. Knowing that Yamamoto would be landing at Ballale at 0745 on a certain day, they sent P-38 fighter planes to arrive at precisely that time. No smart Japanese, the British staff told us, could fail to recognize that the planes' arrival time was more than just coincidence. They were right; the Japanese duly changed their code.[4] It was three weeks before the Americans broke the new code, which cost them three weeks of military advantage at a crucial crossroads in the war. That disadvantage and the risk that the United States might not have been able to break a new Japanese code greatly outweighed the significance of killing Yamamoto, our instructors insisted.

Each morning, MI-6 received and shared with X-2 translations of hundreds of German wireless messages from the day before.[5] The documents were labeled "Most Secret" by the British and "Top-Secret U" by us Americans. That designation was so restricted that most military personnel did not even know it existed. Typically, German *Abwehr* officers or agents in occupied lands radioed Berlin each night about concluded or planned operations. The Germans lived and breathed details. A typical message might speak of recruiting a Frenchman as a German agent, give his real name, false name, and occupation, and describe his mission and method of operation. It was this type of golden information we were to use in tracking German stay-behind agents in France.

The British also indoctrinated us into the secret of Operation Double Cross, their masterful doubling of German agents in England. Sir John Masterman, the Oxford don who devised the double-cross system, described its sweeping objectives as follows:[6]

- ✦ To control the enemy's system
- ✦ To catch spies
- ✦ To learn as much as possible about the personalities and methods of the *Abwehr* and other German intelligence bodies
- ✦ To make German codes and ciphers reveal their secrets
- ✦ To study the questions asked by the Germans as evidence of their intentions
- ✦ To influence their plans by the answers sent back
- ✦ To deceive the enemy about Allied plans

In a darkly lit auditorium, a high-ranking domestic intelligence (MI-5) officer delivered a theatrical explanation of how the British had protected England against German spies during the Battle of Britain in 1940 and thereafter. The Germans had placed *Abwehr* spies in England before the war. When the *Abwehr* started communicating with these agents by radio, they used the German hand-cipher code. Through their intercepts of these ISOS messages, the British located all existing and future incoming German agents.[7]

I remember one spectacular example. MI-5 learned that a German submarine planned to deposit an agent on a remote beach in western England on a pitch-black night. Sure enough, a rubber dinghy dropped him off at the assigned time. Several British operatives emerged from the shelter of the cliffs along the rocky beach, apprehended the man and announced, "Jacob Friedrich, we know you're a German agent posing as Roger Smith, tailor, in Birmingham, with offices at 45 Hull Street. We have friends inside the *Abwehr*. We know all about you and your assignment. Come with us and meet your fate." The agent quivered with fear, expecting to be shot. After letting him sweat for a while, his captors offered to spare his life. All he had to do was cooperate by transmitting misleading messages fed to him by the British back to Germany. Agents who did not cooperate were imprisoned or quietly executed.

In this manner, twenty German agents were doubled either briefly or for the war's duration. Of course, the messages they transmitted had to be fashioned in such a way as to fool the receivers in Germany. For example, as Yale historian Robin Winks wrote, "Messages planted on the Germans had to be cautious and clever; believable, enticing, the kind of information an agent might be expected to obtain, just marginally contradictory between agents, since they reasonably would be expected to learn different 'facts,' and above all, never compromising the Ultra secret itself."[8]

In early 1944, before the Allied invasion of France, many double agents sent messages with false information back to Hamburg or Berlin. Their central theme was that the Allies, under Gen. George Patton, whom the Germans considered to be America's finest general, would invade the French coast near Calais,[9] a long distance from the Normandy beaches where they were actually to land. Hitler was completely duped; the Allies landed in Normandy instead, and Patton remained in England for another month. Even after the surprise Hitler countermanded the movement of four to six armored divisions from the Fifteenth Army near Calais to the beachhead at Normandy, believing that the landing there was just a feint to divert troops from an attack to be launched later by Patton at Calais.[10] It never came. Patton popped up in Normandy a month after the landing, when the beachhead was secure, broke through the German lines, and raced to Paris.

All of us in X-2 were duly impressed by British intelligence's spectacular achievements with Enigma, Ultra, and Double Cross. We were inspired to make X-2—or V-48, as the British referred to us because of the then forty-eight states—a top-notch counterespionage branch. This goal came close to being compromised, it seemed, when in October 1944 Pearson reported to us that the Germans had captured an X-2 major wandering near the front lines in Luxembourg. If tortured, would he disclose our vital secrets? Almost immediately, General Eisenhower issued an order that X-2 personnel (or all OSS personnel, I forget which) were not to venture closer to the front than thirty miles. As it turned out, the major outfoxed his captors, revealed nothing, and was killed only when American bombers attacked his hospital.[11] The order stuck, much to my disappointment, because I had hoped to fly to France and see the action.

4

COUNTERESPIONAGE
ROOKIE

AFTER OWEN KEELING INVITED ME TO STAY AT HIS HOME, I approached OSS headquarters for permission and was told that officers could reside wherever they chose. And so I called on him the next day at his attractive two-story brick home at 61 Murray Road, Wimbledon. There he fed me dinner and, to use his own words, "threw me into bed at one o'clock, after we had talked for hours." By October 9 I had moved all my few belongings to Wimbledon and settled into my home away from home.

Owen Keeling was a delightful Englishman, the director of a company that imported bananas from Jamaica, where he had been born in 1885 and where his ancestors owned sugar plantations. When he was six months old, his father died, and at the age of five he was sent to boarding school in Wimbledon. After he graduated from Cambridge University as an engineer, his stepfather sent him to Canada to work and "clear his head" of academic ideas. He met my newly married parents in Montreal in 1909, where my father was working as superintendent of construction for Carrere and Hastings, the New York architectural firm that had designed the New York Public Library.

I first heard the Keeling name at Christmas at our home in Westport, Connecticut, during the 1920s. With great fanfare, my father placed a piece of paper in the fireplace, explaining that it was a mortgage he had just repaid. Custom required one to burn mortgages when paid off, he said. A nice Englishman, Owen Keeling, had lent him money to replace savings lost when a Canadian bank failed. Keeling said he was obliged to make the unsolicited loan because "the British Empire had let a Yank down by permitting a Canadian bank to fail." In 1940 my mother had offered to house his three daughters in our small five-bedroom house when London was ablaze during the Blitz, but Keeling declined because his wife and two daughters had been removed from London and the middle daughter, Josephine (Jo), kept house for him.

Owen Keeling turned out to be witty, warm, intelligent, well read, and thoughtful, in short, the true English gentleman. Having grown up during Queen Victoria's reign, he was also a bit conservative. He insisted that when I was in his home overnight during his absence on fire-warden duty, chaperones be brought in to protect the reputation of Jo, a warm, energetic, Wimbledon school teacher.

Wimbledon was a forty-five-minute commute by underground or railroad to OSS offices in the heart of London. I planned to stay there for two weeks, until sent on to France, but that assignment was canceled, and so I stayed on for three months. The Keeling home was comfortable in all respects but one: the central heating had been shut off to conserve fuel, and I had to boil water each morning to shave.

Owen Keeling declined my offer to pay for breakfasts and occasional dinners at his home, reporting the event to my mother in his usual witty fashion:

> Every now and then he trots out some silly suggestion that he should pay something towards the house which I easily parry by asking him how much you charged me for the many meals I took in Montreal. This flattens him out. It appears that he and Jo have cooked up some arrangement between them that honour is to be satisfied by his paying for his washing! As a matter of fact, we do very well out of him. For some obscure and doubtless quite unjust reason he gets double meat rations, which goes into our pot. When he came here first he used to expect second helpings. We had lots of fun getting that idea out of his head. It's now so finally out of his head that he frequently doesn't come for supper. He gets it in town—whereby we benefit! I've wondered whether that is really his bright idea.[1]

In January 1945, to avoid the long commute, I moved from the Keeling's to join other OSS officers in a West End flat previously rented to Leslie Howard, the English actor. I wrote home,

> Despite the celebrated English ability for civil service administration, little can be said for the control of rents. English friends tell me very frankly that the price of a flat doubles if you wear the *American* uniform and that's that.

The high rent was offset by the fact that I, as a second lieutenant, receive the equivalent or slightly more than a British major. So there is rough equity.

In the third week of January, Owen received a food package addressed to me and promptly forwarded it, with the following letter:

I hope this will reach you as the office from which Eisenhower, through you, directs the Western and also possibly the Russian war is so very secret; but perhaps the Post Office may be able to find it out. In the Post Office I place my implicit trust.

Last night there reached me a super package from Gristede Bros. Inc. of New York, a delightful parcel of foodstuffs. My greedy self and my greedy daughter thought, "This is fine," until we opened the parcel and there amongst the various goodies in a little envelope addressed to me in your mother's painfully printed handwriting, was a card saying that this is "With Greetings from neighbors of Dick Cutler—Mr. and Mrs. Dudley L. Wadsworth of Westport, Conn." This card was not at all well received because it clearly indicated that the foodstuffs were by no means expected to be eaten by the Keelings alone, but were to be devoured, at least in part, by one Cutler.

Therefore, if you can cough up an address that is not so unalterably hush-hush and holy, we will send you an extremely small part of the contents of the parcel. It has been suggested by the friend who is taking down this letter that she thinks that I have no right whatever to any part of the parcel and that it is entirely meant for you. I beg to enter a demurrer.

In mid-October, after my indoctrination in the British system of intercepting and decoding German messages, Norman Pearson asked Washington to transfer me to his jurisdiction. I was to be shifted from the Mediterranean theater of operations to the European theater for duty on the French desk in London. Pearson cited a desperate shortage of special combat intelligence (SCI) personnel in northern France. Washington agreed.

I started working on the French desk tracing German agents in France. The inter-theater shift had good and bad technical consequences. It delayed my overdue promotion to first lieutenant,[2] which rankled me because OSS shortly increased my level of responsibility well above my rank, making my job more difficult than necessary. On the other hand, the army's blissfully slow channels took several months to cancel my seven-dollars-a-day luxury allowance, granted for living in London while technically assigned to the Mediterranean theater.

Thereafter, Pearson periodically talked of sending me to Paris or Metz to assist an SCI team "made up of British and American officers which was to deal with stay-behind networks in France."[3] SCI teams received from X-2 London translations of all intercepted wireless messages from nearby German agents reporting to their headquarters. These intercepts often identified an agent by pseudonym and place of operation. SCI would track the agent down and either eliminate him or persuade him to become a double agent. The intercepted German messages identified 3,575 agents in Western Europe.[4] No doubt that large number accounted for Pearson's concern that his counterespionage forces were undermanned.

Two weeks later, in late October, Pearson called me into his office looking very purposeful. Ignoring the ash accumulating on the tip of his cigarette, he launched into one of the exact analyses for which he was famous:

> I've examined the situation in Europe. Patton has moved so rapidly across France that we'll be in Germany sooner than expected. X-2 has too few German-speaking officers for work there. X-2 could hire more linguists, but we believe it wiser to take a thoroughly trained intelligence officer, like you, and ask him to learn German. I consulted with Harvard and Yale German professors here. They advise that, with your current French and Spanish, plus earlier six years of Latin, you can learn German in four months, if tutored. We've engaged a Berlitz tutor for you. You're to give learning German a high priority, but still work at the French desk during the day.

What was I going to do with my newly acquired language? Pearson read my mind. "You'll start memorizing the names of the top four hundred German intelligence officers and every member of their immediate families. Once you've mastered German, you can be posted to General Omar Bradley's headquarters at the Twelfth Army Group." Bradley was commander of U.S. armies in northern Europe. "After the United States occupies Germany, you can help G-2 and the Counterintelligence Corps (CIC) run down *Abwehr* and *Sicherheitsdienst* officers as they attempt to go underground."

Pearson believed the German intelligence officers were most likely to hide out with parents or relatives, especially those who lived in remote mountainous areas. I should search out such locations in the officers' biographies. It was a tall order,[5] but because research and organizing tedious details are what young lawyers do better than anything else, I considered the massive job doable.

While Pearson was shifting my assignment within OSS, I was exploring a change in my postwar career. Should I leave Donovan's Wall Street law firm to become a foreign correspondent? I had written a dozen articles for the *Bridgeport Post Telegram* about my impressions of South America while touring there in 1941 after graduation from law school. But what really kindled my desire was meeting a correspondent for *Time* magazine, Bill Bayless, in London. Other attorneys in OSS-London, noting that most OSS people drawn from Donovan, Leisure, Newton, and Lumbard were now majors or colonels, had concluded that my low rank would prejudice my future advancement at the law firm. No doubt that would have been a short-term disadvantage, but the logic impressed me back then. I yearned for adventure, and my fingers itched for the typewriter.

I conferred often with reporters, in particular Bill Bayless, who had been Berlin bureau chief for *Time* before the war. Bayless and several other reputable reporters said that I would have no trouble at all becoming a foreign correspondent in view of my three foreign languages, my career up until then, and the fact that some war correspondents were burned out and planning to quit after the war.

On Pearson's instructions I started lessons in German, two hours a day with a petite, ultra-polite, Viennese refugee in her forties who was an excellent tutor. Nights were spent toiling over vocabulary and writing. German was hard, but fun, to learn. My instructress drilled me in pronunciation, grammar, and the gender and declension of nouns, whose nominative, possessive, dative, and accusative forms resembled Latin's. I made progress, but questioned the confident professors' forecast that in four months' time I would speak, read, and write adequate German.

As I labored over the language and started memorizing the names and ranks of top German officers, the assignment took on new significance. Repeatedly, at weekly meetings in which Pearson delivered strategic summaries, we heard talk of German plans to build a redoubt in the Alps where they would fight; later they would go underground as the French Resistance had done. They would organize small groups of "werewolves" to emerge at night and assassinate Allied occupation troops. During these sessions there was loose talk about OSS's training assassins to kill Herman Göring, the flamboyant *Luftwaffe* chief, and other Nazi leaders.

At these briefings, Pearson was in top form. A spectacular ham, he savored every step in the unraveling of a plot and couldn't resist embellishing his presentation with wild gesticulations. As described by a Yale historian, "He began his briefings, without notes, from behind his desk; soon he would sit upon it; and then he would progress to the top of the safe, to the window sill, in constant movement, a giant foulard handkerchief hanging down his chest, witty and complex material flowing from him."[6] An avid smoker, he would let his cigarette ash grow as he talked on. We sat there transfixed, wondering where the ashes would land when they finally fell off, and whether this habit of his was histrionics or sheer self-absorption with his briefing.

Meanwhile, in November 1944, the western advance slowed and the Germans dug in. On December 16 Hitler launched a whirlwind counterattack in the Ardennes forest. Dubbed "Autumn Mist" by Hitler, it became known as the Battle of the Bulge to us because on a map the advance looked like a large bulge protruding into Belgium. Whatever the name, the counterattack caught the Allies by surprise. Before the attack the Germans had scrupulously observed radio silence, using telephones whenever possible, instead of wireless. That precaution dried up the stream of Ultra intercepts of wireless instructions to German troops. Furthermore, bad weather grounded Allied aerial reconnaissance, while German divisions, despite heavy snow, barreled forward.

At first, Gen. Omar Bradley underestimated German intentions. Fortunately, Eisenhower overruled both Bradley and an equally unalarmed General Patton and promptly started countermeasures.[7] Veteran German troops overran some of the heavily outnumbered American troops, many of whom had not yet seen combat.[8] Eventually, however, more seasoned American troops and strong counterattacks by Patton's soldiers from the south and Bernard Montgomery's soldiers from the north stopped the German advance.[9]

OSS SCI teams in France used double agents to mislead the Germans into believing that Patton's troops were two days farther along their route than they actually were. Lawrence de Neufville, a brilliant, colorful, SCI team member located south of the battle, reported that wireless messages from doubled agents, received by their Germans before they had blacked out wireless communications, were "extremely useful." The messages were short, simple, and informative; for example: "Stay-behind agent Leon established in a farm cottage 12 kilometers north of Amiens on RN 78." De Neufville recounted the following in a letter to me:[10]

We received the decoded messages in France via one-time OSS code. It was up to field personnel like me to find the agent by a seemingly haphazard and random search (in order not to disclose our ability to decode). The agent then had to be persuaded to serve as a double agent (not difficult because he could be told truthfully that the French would shoot him if he were handed over). Using the suitcase radio, the captured agent would then be used for deception (which had to be worked out with the designated officer in G-2). If deception was kept simple enough, and especially if it recounted as facts observations that became fact shortly after, then it could be highly useful. Example: in the Battle of the Bulge, the enemy was persuaded that Patton's troops coming from the south were two days ahead of the real possibility simply by having the agent report the correct bumper numbers of units that had not yet reached his observation point.

The most remarkable thing occurred when we captured the German headquarters that imagined it was controlling SCI's agents. Every single one of their reports was recorded as genuine. This can be used as a good boast for the SCI teams, and undoubtedly was. More likely (I think) their headquarters simply ignored or suppressed any doubts because it was much safer, vis-à-vis Himmler [the head of all German intelligence and police forces], to say 'Our stay-behind agents were a resounding success' than it would have been to say 'Many of our agents were captured by the enemy' . . . as reflected in the fact that the validity of their reports was always doubtful.

As the battle quickened the Germans resumed wireless transmissions, and Montgomery was substantially aided by a fistful of Ultra intercepts of messages from two Panzer armies disclosing their intentions and weak points.[11]

Meanwhile, the largest European battle in which the United States had participated put a damper on confident talk of a quick end to the war. Troops at the front lacked appropriate clothing and suffered terribly from the cold weather. In London we were ordered to surrender jackets that had insulated us from the fifty-degree air in OSS offices. They were sent to the front and not replaced. The jackets, we remarked, shouldn't have been issued to us in the first place if the troops hadn't received any.

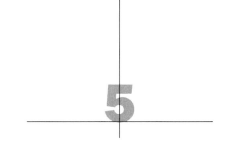

LONDON AT WAR

WHILE ALLIED ARMIES WERE FIGHTING THE GERMAN ARMY ON THE continent, I had a ringside seat watching how London fared. Upon my arrival in October 1944, I expected to see a devastated city. We had been accustomed in the United States to newspaper photographs of two stereotyped London war scenes: rescue teams pulling wounded and dead from collapsed structures, and appalling nighttime fires raging out of control. Instead, I found that most buildings were still standing, although they looked grim for lack of paint and prolonged exposure to coal soot, and that the destruction was concentrated in the dock area of the lower Thames, far to the east of St. Paul's and the Tower of London. Destroying the docks had been the German bombers' primary objective during the Blitz of 1940 to 1941.[1]

The borough of Westminster and the fashionable Mayfair section, miles west, suffered less. That was where the British government was located—Parliament, Whitehall, and Downing Street—as were Eisenhower's Supreme Headquarters of the Allied Expeditionary Force (SHAEF), the U.S. embassy, and OSS. To be sure, Parliament had been hit and was partly boarded up, but its scars were minor compared to the gaping open basements along Bond and Oxford streets, where intermittent buildings had been bombed out.[2] By the time I arrived, the streets were filled once again with handsome, black, English taxis and milling pedestrians. The Battle of Britain was ancient history to a country that had subsequently struggled valiantly through four grueling years of war and deprivation.[3]

The *Luftwaffe* had halted the Blitz on May 16, 1941—five weeks before Germany invaded Russia—and didn't attack London again until January 1944, when it resumed greatly weakened air raids that lasted until April

1944.[4] What lay next in store became apparent in June, just after the Allied invasion at Normandy, when the Germans first launched long-range terror weapons against London, V-1s (buzz bombs), followed by V-2s (rockets) in September. Nightly bomb and rocket attacks were vicious evidence of Hitler's reaction to heavy British and American bombing of German cities.

The pilotless buzz bomb was the ultimate weapon of terror, sounding "much like a sewing machine in the distance, followed by a long moment of utter, eerie silence (when the motor cut out and the flying bomb turned 180 degrees and dove toward the earth) and then an explosion that sounded exactly like a gas main blowing up."[5] The V-2s were forty-seven-foot-long rockets that shot as high as seventy miles into the sky over Holland, then descended noiselessly on London, faster than the speed of sound, to unleash a one-ton payload. V-2s could not be heard until after the explosion.

One night as I was walking to Owen Keeling's home in Wimbledon, the sky exploded with light. I counted some twenty seconds until the sound came, accompanied by a blast of wind, and calculated from the speed of sound that the rocket had landed near Hyde Park many miles away. In the morning I learned that was exactly where it hit, next to Selfridge's department store on Oxford Street. Buzz bombs terrorized an office mate of mine at OSS, a Czech refugee who had been living in London for some time and whose nerves were frayed as a result. Each time a buzz bomb put-putted overhead, he would throw himself down on the floor and cover his face, worried that the window next to his desk would explode, spewing shards of glass every which way.

Over 2,300 V-1s rained down on London between June 1944 and March 1945, when Allied armies overran their launching sites, and some 500 V-2 rockets hit the city between September 1944 and late March 1945.[6] As a result 6,080 Londoners were killed and 40,000 wounded. The attacks were nerve-wracking, to be sure, but the American papers made them sound much more destructive than they really were. I tried to reassure my family in a letter on February 14, 1945:

> V-bombs and rockets are exaggerated in the N.Y. press. Correspondents must sell sensation and even staid Anne Hare McMormick of the *Times* makes London sound like a cripple. In fact, London buzzes imperturbably about its way. . . . What we can say about V bombs (because of censorship) would fit neatly on the back of a postage stamp. . . . Since you can hear

buzz bombs a long distance—maybe 15 miles—it's more a question of noise than anything else.

What bothered those of us in X-2 more than the bombs was the intense, damp cold of unheated offices and continual blackouts. Our office temperature often dipped to 50 degrees Fahrenheit. Fog seeped through the cracks in the old building, preventing anyone seeing from one end of a corridor to the other. Outside on the street we had great difficulty navigating in the fog during a blackout. Reaching a specific address under these conditions was like trying to locate a trail on a remote mountain without a flashlight, matches, or compass. Once I missed a hotel restaurant three times and later found that I had been just a few feet away from the entrance.

London showed the effects of the long war. Not only were buildings unpainted and drab, but stocks were scarce. We often spent two hours a day traipsing from one empty store to another. I was impressed at how the English gritted their teeth and muddled through. They bore the strain well, complaining primarily about the blackout. Most of them worked Sundays and took time off during the week to shop, enduring long queues and many disappointments. Shops in wintertime closed around four to allow their keepers to get home before dark.

I saw the most striking evidence of stolid English pluck in the underground. There, homeless and frightened families slept at night. The trains ran until 11:45 PM. Men and women, and some children (most children had been sent out of London), lay on wicker bunks or on the pavement, trying to sleep while trains whizzed by and people walked around their heads. The English were making a big effort to repair and rebuild the damaged homes of London by importing thousands of laborers from the countryside, but it was a massive job, and meanwhile the continued bombing weakened the foundations of homes.

The English were more law-abiding than we freewheeling Americans. They also resisted social change, even under extraordinary pressure. Neither the immense burden of war nor the noble cause for which it was being waged—democracy—could loosen the English class system, kept in place by telltale accents that disclosed people's social station. Although it was said the class system was breaking down, I saw poor families on trains who were afraid to sit in first class when there was no sitting room in third class—"because it isn't right, you know"—and who rode standing for eight hours.

Despite the hardships of the war, London had a lighter side. It was, after all, the theater capital of the world. The English defiantly and triumphantly continued to flock to their beloved theaters. While museums carted away or covered up their treasured statues, paintings, and artifacts, theaters basked in the glow of government subsidies and boosted morale after years of war. Audiences coped with chilly interiors by bundling up in warm clothes and sipping hot coffee at their seats. The small size of the theaters created the illusion that the actors were talking to you personally.

Almost as soon as I arrived, I started taking dates to plays, which started early because of the difficulty of traversing London under blackout conditions and during nighttime bomb attacks. I usually wangled the best seats, those in the "stalls," in the front of the orchestra. In "double summertime," when wartime London stayed light until 7:00 PM in February, my date and I could travel to the theater by daylight, often on foot or partway by tube. After the performance, in blackout conditions, we would stumble our way to dinner by following thin strips of luminescent yellow paint carefully applied to each sidewalk curb. In fog, we were permitted to use a "torch," or flashlight, provided we pointed it down at the yellow strip.

Plays in London cost much less than in New York, even less than American movies playing in London, and as a result I attended all sorts of productions, classical and modern, tragic and comic—Shakespeare, Shaw, Maugham, Sheridan, Congreve, Ibsen, and Chekhov. I saw every play in London, some twenty-seven in all, crowding them into the periods before and after February and March, when my workload skyrocketed. John Gielgud, Ralph Richardson, Laurence Olivier—the giant thespians of the twentieth century—were in their early primes. We Americans came to appreciate the British way of training actors, who master their art in the provinces before ascending to the London stage—just as American baseball players first train in the minor leagues.

The audiences were mostly English. U.S. airmen seldom attended the theater. Many who made the difficult trip to London from their bases in East Anglia came to town primarily to cruise around Piccadilly Circus—London's Times Square—where they picked up well-painted and willing English girls. The British were shocked by the Americans' public necking, which had become so prevalent that in the spring of 1944 Eisenhower issued an order forbidding it. The ban had no apparent effect on visiting air crews, who feared a fling in London might be their last before getting shot down over Germany.

The English joked about the Yanks being "overpaid, oversexed, and over here." Others enjoyed telling us, "Bad luck for the Yanks that they were the last overseas troops here. The Poles were the first, and they had a terrible reputation. The Canadians came and raised so much hell, we forgot about the Poles. Then you Yanks came, and we don't remember either the Canadians or the Poles now. But there's no one to come after the Yanks. You are out of luck."

In addition to American promiscuity, the English had another pet peeve: the excessive granting of military medals to American soldiers. The English said the medals made them look too much like Reichsmarschall Hermann Göring, whose repulsively fat chest above a corseted belly was bedecked with fancy Nazi ribbons. I sympathized with the English on this score. After all, British general Bernard Montgomery's boys, who defeated German Gen. Erwin Rommel at El Alamein in Britain's first military victory of the war, only got medals after Parliament practically threatened to blow the War Ministry into the Thames. No British soldier was allowed more than one medal.

The presence of American troops was more distasteful to the upper than the lower class. In addition to the American tendency to pick up girls in London and take them to fashionable hotels, the upper class privately deplored the lack of decorum, for example, when Americans would slouch against buildings with their hands in their pockets. By contrast, the poorer people of England showed a warm appreciation for Americans, not least because they helped break down the strong social customs that bound the under class. Cockneys told me that American soldiers were responsible for changing the convention of dividing a pub into three areas, each for a separate stratum of society. My English barber remarked on how frank and good-humored the Americans were: "We English, we're a bit stiff, you know. I like your direct remarks and Yank humor. You've been good for our country."

Living with an English family in Wimbledon and working daily with MI-6 gave me a prized exposure to the English at work and play. I quickly learned that the educated among them were whizzes at the liberal arts. This small class of people that ran England's social and political life (52 percent of Parliament went to public school, while only 2 percent of the country did) were well versed in drama, public speaking, history, and the arts, well read, broad-minded, enjoyable, and sensible. Their social outlook was more conservative than that of their American counterparts, but they were less rabid about their beliefs. I never heard Tories wax as apoplectic about Labour Party leaders as did Republicans about Roosevelt's key advisors. The British were more composed and less bitter.

Civil servants I worked with took pride in their jobs, were fastidiously accurate in what they reported, and seemed usually anxious to help. At a public debate I had a chance to express my admiration for the English civil service. Owen Keeling and I often argued about politics and in particular the British Empire, which he stoutly defended. He introduced me to an English debating society, the Brain Trust, in order to let me present the American view on India (that it should be given its independence), which he considered erroneous. Four of us sat behind a table, while the audience shot us questions about India (which became independent two years later) and the comparative value of American and British education and foreign policy. The Brain Trust members each gave his view, then the audience replied. It was smoothly conducted, and we all enjoyed it immensely. This was my only public opportunity to express to the British my admiration for their effort and their pluck through the long, grim years of war.

In January I was invited by Mrs. Randolph Churchill, later Mrs. Averell Harriman, U.S. ambassador to France, to join the Churchill Club, an honor probably extended to Americans whose affection for Great Britain the English wished to cultivate. The club, located in the Dean's Yard at Westminster Cathedral next to Parliament, listed Winston Churchill as president. Its mission was to "provide a fitting centre for our American and Dominion friends who are interested in all aspects of Britain which are of enduring value and beauty, and form the cherished heritage of the English-speaking peoples."[7] Twice a week, the club presented recitals and lectures by such intellectual heavyweights as Geoffrey Crowther, editor of the London *Economist*, humorist A. P. Herbert, and the American expatriate poet T. S. Eliot.

Through one of the Churchill Club's officers, Brendan Bracken, a member of Parliament who was close to Churchill, I once procured two passes to sit in the visitors' gallery at Parliament. My friend Jane, a beautiful devotee of the arts who worked in the X-2 German section, and I attended a debate on whether to back a right-wing or left-wing government in liberated Greece. Our view could not have been finer. Jane was ushered into Clementine Churchill's seat and sat there somewhat apprehensively lest the rightful owner show up when her husband made his appearance. As it turned out, the great man didn't attend the session, nor did his wife. However, Anthony Eden, the dapper foreign secretary, did show and amazed us by slouching forward in his seat and propping his feet on the center table. The discussion was heated. Members of the extreme left lashed out, calling the prime minister a liar and a reactionary. It was a display of acrimony that would have roiled the floor of the comparatively calm U.S. Senate. The British could be reserved, but inside the walls of Parliament, all their inhibitions evaporated.

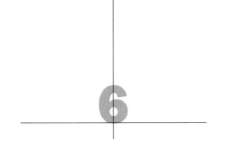

AMERICAN SPIES
IN GERMANY

The Allies' costly failure to detect Hitler's 250,000-man Ardennes offensive in advance quickly persuaded OSS to intensify its efforts to infiltrate agents into Germany. When the Allied response was floundering in December, Major General Donovan put William J. Casey in charge of Special Intelligence in London.[1] Casey was a hard-driving thirty-two-year-old attorney, destined to become director of the CIA under President Ronald Reagan.

Though months earlier Special Intelligence had decided to infiltrate agents into Germany,[2] the British discouraged the effort and initially wouldn't permit OSS to fly agents from England into Germany. The agents, the Brits argued, wouldn't be able to penetrate the Nazis' tightly controlled society without the support of a strong local resistance.[3] Moreover, the British felt, their Ultra wireless intercepts had already brought them unparalleled intelligence about German military and diplomatic plans—they didn't need more.

British skepticism notwithstanding, OSS had placed three active agents inside Germany in the fall of 1944. In September, with the help of the RAF, OSS–Special Operations parachuted a German socialist émigré on the Gestapo's death list into the Ruhr Valley. Four months later his wife, outfitted as a Red Cross nurse, made a trip from Switzerland to his safe house in the Ruhr and brought back his thirteen-page report on the potential for a German Socialist resistance. He also identified bombing targets such as the giant I. G. Farbenindustrie chemical factory and an electric power plant near Cologne. Both were subsequently bombed.

Also in September, Allen Dulles, based in Berne, Switzerland, sent Fritz

Molden over the Swiss border to Vienna to organize an Austrian resistance. Molden, once imprisoned for anti-Nazi activities in Vienna, had later deserted the German Army in Italy, then linked up with Italian partisans, before crossing into Switzerland and being introduced to Dulles. A bold, charismatic man, he was successful in his attempt to kindle a resistance movement. Molden became a Viennese publisher after the war.

In November a White Russian opportunist traveled for OSS from France to Berlin, passing himself off as a member of the German *Sicherheitsdienst* assigned to spy on Russian émigré groups in Paris. He walked through the German mine fields opposite the American Seventh Army with help arranged by Henry B. Hyde, a French-born American, educated in English schools and at Harvard, who was the most versatile OSS officer in France.[4] The agent fooled two *Sicherheitsdienst* interrogators with his carefully constructed cover story.

But placing OSS agents in Germany was a dangerous business. A fourth agent arrived safely in Germany in December, but was captured the following January by the Gestapo while traveling to join the German socialist agent in the Ruhr. OSS canceled a fifth agent's mission when X-2 discovered that he was a member of the die-hard Nazi *Schutz Staffel* (SS), posing as a captured anti-Nazi soldier.

OSS imaginatively solved the knotty problem of recruiting agents least likely to be detected inside Germany. Most Americans of German extraction being too big a risk—they weren't familiar with Germany and would arouse suspicion, not being in the German Army—OSS sought to recruit German prisoners and émigrés, including Communists, as well as Dutch, French, Belgian, and White Russians, who could pose as one of the three million foreign workers in Germany.

Meanwhile, Eisenhower's headquarters asked OSS to investigate numerous military targets inside Germany, even a stretch of new autobahn from which Hitler's dreaded new ME-262 jet fighters were supposedly being launched.

In January 1945, OSS faced two major obstacles to parachuting agents into Germany and enabling them to transmit intelligence back safely and promptly. The U.S. Eighth Air Force and the RAF resisted assigning their faster planes and valuable pilots to single-plane, hazardous night flights deep into Germany. Antiaircraft fire and German night fighters posed a threat. At first the Eighth Air Force wouldn't fly spy missions north of Stuttgart and east of Munich, which limited OSS operations to the less militarily significant southwest quadrant of Germany. The unavailability of air transport, compounded by a long spell of bad weather, delayed parachute drops, while teams of agents and radiomen stood anxiously by. Finally, after tense, sometimes bitter, negotiations, OSS-London persuaded the Eighth Air Force to add fast RAF Mosquito and American A-26 bombers for spy missions to fly over all of Germany. The A-26 could dive at 425 miles per hour through ack-ack fire in Holland, then hedgehop below German radar for several hundred miles to Berlin.

A larger obstacle to effective missions was the substantial risk of detection by Germany's ground-based mobile radio finders. Their range of twenty miles would quickly zero in on any agent sending portable-radio broadcasts back to England. OSS-London solved the problem when Stephen H. Simpson Jr., who had served as a Radio Corporation of America (RCA) scientist in New York, developed the "Joan-Eleanor" system. An agent on the ground would transmit by wireless voice radio through a narrow band directly up to an airplane circling overhead. The radio was like a specialized cell phone fifty years ahead of its time, except that it weighed four pounds. The message could be recorded and even played back for verification.[5] These state-of-the-art broadcasts were never detected by the enemy.

Despite the obstacles, eventually nearly two hundred OSS agents infiltrated Germany from all directions.[6] Many parachuted in, while others merely walked across the borders. Approximately fifty additional agents sought their way through German minefields in front of the U.S. Seventh Army near the Rhine, south of Strasbourg. Two-thirds were killed going or returning, a horrendous loss that Henry Hyde halved by later parachuting agents in fifty to sixty miles behind the lines.[7] These agents would investigate German military activity in areas pinpointed by the Seventh Army before returning through the minefields.

Dropping agents into Berlin presented a special challenge because of its distance—580 miles from England—and the fierce antiaircraft fire. On March 1, 1945, two native Berliners, both Communists, parachuted into a field thirty miles west of the city and made their way to the home of one of the agent's parents. The agents later radioed up to the plane overhead that a certain power plant continued to supply energy to munitions factories. It was subsequently bombed. Toward the end of the war, the same Berlin OSS team reported that Hitler's powerful number-two man, Heinrich Himmler, had slipped out of the city in the direction of Hamburg.

As the war ground on, OSS parachuted many agents into remote areas such as Munich, Innsbruck, and the approaches to the Brenner Pass through which trains carried supplies to the German Army in Italy. OSS teams near Munich located a jet aircraft factory and ammunition trains, which were promptly bombed by the U.S. Fifteenth Air Force, based in Italy, nearer than the Eighth Air Force in England.

Two Belgian OSS agents who parachuted into five feet of snow in the high Alps near Kitzbühl were joined there by three German deserters, who helped them organize the growing Austrian Resistance and identify bomb targets. Their fifty radio reports resulted in many successful bomb runs by the Fifteenth Air Force.

One German-born American Jew with a Schwabian accent, Fred Mayer, parachuted into Austria. A master of four languages, he disguised himself first as a German officer living in an office's caserne, and then, when his cover wore thin, as a French foreign worker. Mayer and his recruits succeeded in identifying not only twenty-six ammunition trains destined for Italy, but also the location and dimensions of Hitler's bunker in Berlin. Ultimately captured and tortured by the Gestapo, he was interrogated by the gauleiter, or local Nazi administrator, and negotiated with him to arrange the surrender of Innsbruck, which saved the lives of advancing American troops. Mayer survived and was recommended for a congressional medal, but did not receive it.

Another OSS team, in Munich, procured the pay records of the local Gestapo and identified all officers and agents, including false names and real addresses.

But the boldest OSS operation ever conceived, Iron Cross, never got started. One hundred men posing as a German mountain infantry company were to parachute into the outskirts of alpine Innsbruck and capture top Nazi leaders. A U.S. Army captain, Aaron Bank, had recruited them for OSS from German anti-Nazi civilians interned by the French and from prisoners of war in France. Most were Communists, and some had fought in the Spanish civil war. Hearing about the mission, Donovan ordered, "Tell Bank to get Hitler." OSS shortly thereafter canceled the mission because the war was approaching its end.[8]

From Stockholm, OSS sent a member of the Danish underground, Hennings Jensen-Schmidt, to Berlin to organize sabotage by foreign workers. He used the apartment of a Swedish resident of Berlin, Karl Wiberg, as a safe house and place to stockpile grenades and rifles.

By March 15 OSS had five sources of information in Berlin: the two Communists broadcasting by Joan Eleanor, the White Russian working for the *Sicherheitsdienst*, the recently arrived Dane, and most important of all, Fritz Kolbe, a highly placed clerk in the German Foreign Office. Kolbe regularly delivered to Allen Dulles in Switzerland the more revealing cables Joachim von Ribbentrop received from German ambassadors and military attachés around the world.

Of the nearly two hundred agents infiltrated into Germany (not including the tactical agents sent through the minefields before the Seventh Army), only thirty-six were captured, killed, or reported missing.[9] For an agent to arrive at his destination without injury and avoid capture, however, was only a first step. Many surviving agents did not manage to report back. Of sixty-two teams of agents dropped from London into Germany by April 7, 1945, only twenty-six succeeded in making contact with OSS, and three of these were suspected of operating under duress following capture.[10] The mission of most agents was to observe military traffic as Allied armies pushed deeper into Germany. Those who reported back often identified military trains that were promptly bombed. In one instance the U.S. Eighth Air Force Command commended an agent for identifying a heavily traveled railroad intersection and making an immediate follow-up report on the success of the ensuing bombardment.

OSS clearly established its ability to infiltrate agents into Germany, a substantial fraction of whom succeeded in pinpointing prime bombing targets such as arms factories or military trains. The results justified the effort. On the other hand, agents who entered Germany late in the war could hardly be expected to unearth the most valuable human intelligence—Hitler's plans, valuable scraps of which Allen Dulles obtained from top-level German insiders. No human intelligence can rival that provided by a defector, a mole inside the enemy's intelligence system, or a long-term agent.

On December 15, 1944, as the Battle of the Bulge was getting under way, Pearson abruptly reassigned me for the second time. I was to recheck, or vet, as the British said, the security of all 750 American agents in Europe and the Middle East. This brought my German lessons to a crashing halt. Pearson's reasons for putting me in a brand-new vetting job varied according to who recorded them. He told me part of the story: "We're going to change your job again. General Donovan is very concerned about possible enemy penetration of OSS. Some seductive Italian member of SIM [Italy's secret service] married a naval intelligence officer. In bed she learned information she couldn't otherwise have easily acquired." Pearson said I could have immediate access to the MI-6 register of all 1.5 million people in Europe whom MI-6 considered to be of security interest. They could be friendly agents, enemy agents, suspicious persons, or pro-German natives. All I had to do was give MI-6's Section V the name of a particular agent, and the British would report to me anything their precious register said about him.

The story of the seductive Italian, if it was even true, was only one of the many reasons for the new job shift. For some time, various sources had been concerned that Secret Intelligence (SI), the "positive," or "offensive," intelligence arm of OSS, and Special Operations (SO), its sabotage arm, might be recruiting an occasional agent who wasn't sufficiently secure. Trustworthiness is indispensable in the professional spy business. OSS was concerned that certain recruiters, in their rush to meet the demands of war by supplying agents, might have undervalued this essential requirement.

Among the most concerned were the British intelligence services, MI-6 and MI-5. They had, they believed, double-checked their agents for weaknesses such as alcoholism, lack of courage, and recklessness about security measures. Influenced by their view of Americans as carefree, naive fellows who took discipline and security too lightly, the British were afraid that the Yanks would jeopardize their spy-free island. The British had painstakingly transmitted false reports about the accuracy of German bombing through doubled *Abwehr* agents in England, causing the Germans to aim a majority of their buzz bombs short of London.[11] Now, the reasoning went, the cavalier cousins from across the Atlantic might recruit some wily German agent and transport him to London for training, where he could observe damage still being inflicted by Hitler's bombs and rockets. When parachuted back into Germany by the Americans, he might report to his German masters, who would then improve the accuracy of their bombardment.

X-2 had long wanted to double-check the security of agents already recruited by SI. The British agencies strongly supported that effort and, in fact, may have even suggested it in the first place. There was just one problem. OSS-SI, which recruited agents for clandestine operations in Europe, was reluctant to surrender the names of its agents to X-2 lest it lose a portion of its independence. The issue went to Donovan as the head of OSS. SI won at first. Later, when the branch carelessly recruited a German agent in Italy, he overruled SI and ordered X-2 Europe, under Pearson, immediately to vet the security of all OSS agents in Europe and the Middle East.[12] The careless recruitment of a German agent must have been a fact that Pearson camouflaged with his fable of an Italian spy marrying a naval intelligence officer.

Pearson was a wily chap. Suspecting that SI might continue to resist Donovan's order by indirect means, he selected me to do the vetting full time, partly because my background as a Wall Street lawyer and a Yale graduate would result in my vetting recommendations being more readily accepted by the hyper-security-sensitive Section V of MI-6 and MI-5. Also, as he later told historians, I was a friend of Bill Donovan's.[13] That opinion was thinly based on my being a very junior member of Donovan's Wall Street law firm while on military leave. Pearson calculated that the appearance of my "friendship" with Donovan would provide backup clout in possible internal fights with SI over vetting. Naturally, he didn't explain his reasoning in the official record. Rather, he dryly attributed his choice to "Cutler's legal training and a reorganization assignment he had accomplished for the Intelligence Division of the Board of Economic Warfare."[14]

After the thoroughly professional British gave me a crash course in vetting, I created X-2's vetting system from scratch. To become an agent, a candidate had to be deemed loyal, discreet, sensible, and courageous, as well as not an alcoholic and not a homosexual—in fact, not vulnerable at all. The more secret an agent's mission, the higher the vetting standards.

My system involved several steps. First, SI and SO had to provide a full dossier on each agent: his curriculum vitae, the history of his recruitment, and a statement by the spymaster as to why he considered the agent to be secure. I quickly learned that it doesn't pay to permit the spymaster to guess what points should be covered in making the case for his proposed agent. Accordingly, I developed forms and repeatedly improved them, which would require the spymaster to deal with all aspects of the agent's security. In May 1945 OSS adopted these forms for use worldwide.

As a matter of routine, I would ask MI-6's Section V for possible information on an agent in their register and compare what MI-6 reported about him with prior SI or SO information. Occasionally, I asked Scotland Yard for possible criminal records on émigré agents who had resided in England before recruitment. Sometimes I asked SI or SO to answer my questions or those coming from the British through me.

I recall rejecting only two or three agents as security risks. One was a former British agent who had been let go because of a perception that he was unreliable, only to be quickly snapped up by an American officer eager to recruit spies. The British suspected he had spilled secrets while in German captivity in Holland before escaping.

Our stricter vetting process reassured the worried English that their American cousins were not totally slaphappy and casual after all. In fact, the greatest value of my work was to restore British confidence that agents imported into England by the Americans had been thoroughly and professionally checked.

Ironically, during this period when the British were so concerned about the security of U.S. intelligence, five Soviet moles, later infamous, occupied high positions in Britain's vaunted MI-6. Of the so-called Cambridge Five, the three most notorious were Guy Burgess and Donald McClean, who fled to Moscow in 1951, and Kim Philby, who had tipped them off that they were under investigation. In 1963 he too fled to Moscow, became a Soviet hero, and later died there.

Soon after my vetting job began, I was flooded with agents' names, often accompanied by frantic requests for immediate clearance. Some agents were completing six months of training for particular targets or missions in Germany, and their airdrops were already scheduled from bases in East Anglia. Everyone wanted me to rush. Often, in turn, I asked Section V to speed things up. Section V was represented by Capt. Blake Budden, whose office was a floor below mine. Crippled during World War I, Budden had a noticeable limp that exacerbated the gruff, peremptory way he handled the OSS staff. He would growl, stomp his foot, and intimidate any secretary I dispatched to his office with a polite request to pick up the pace. Soon I began relaying the requests myself, taking him to lunch, and sending him and his wife small presents specially ordered from the United States. This vastly improved his cooperation.

Despite Blake Budden's help in expediting answers to my urgent requests, my work escalated, and by late February 1945, as the Allies prepared to cross the Rhine into Germany, I was putting in one hundred hours a week.

7

CLEARING AGENTS BEFORE
THE RHINE CROSSING

In February 1945 Eisenhower's armies slogged through mud and determined German resistance and at the end of the first week of March reached the Rhine. As noted, once back inside Germany the *Wehrmacht* communicated mostly by way of telephone, depriving the Allies of their former advantage of learning German military intentions through intercepted wireless messages. This loss intensified the need for OSS agents behind German lines.

As the number of agents awaiting clearance mounted, OSS slowly acted to help me, increasing my staff to five secretaries—and briefly in March, to six—to solicit, receive, record, cross-check, and transmit the flow of data from our OSS branches to Section V of MI-6, Scotland Yard, and other outside agencies. The secretaries typed every spy's biography and many cross-references to facilitate rapid and thorough cross-checking. All this was in the precomputer age. One or two secretaries with computers would do the job better and more rapidly today than six, who had only typewriters and carbon paper (for duplicates), did back then.

Cables had to be sent to OSS-Washington recommending clearance or nonclearance. To expedite matters, OSS X-2 authorized me to sign cables "in the clear," that is, without the delay caused by using my code name. Encoding required that a message be taken to the code section, which sometimes had competing customers. Likewise, any questions or rejections were communicated uncoded to SI or SO. When I reported that an agent was not yet cleared or, rarely, had been turned down as a security risk, the agent's controller, sometimes an army colonel, would be outraged. I got calls at all hours of the day or night at the office or my spacious West End flat demanding or protesting action. I never gave in to angry demands to clear an agent prematurely or to clear one who had been rejected.

The British enforced my orders indirectly. They refused to permit American planes to leave British airfields with a registered alien or spy unless I had cleared that person. OSS officers bringing agents to the airport without my clearance were bluntly told the alien would not leave until "Cutler approves." I was supposed to get—or tried in the name of prudence to get—Pearson's okay on unpopular delays or refusals, but his schedule was busy and erratic. Sometimes I had no choice but to act on my own, regardless of my low military rank, which had recently edged up to first lieutenant after thirteen months of hard work. Occasionally, Pearson and I managed to meet at midnight. Once he lambasted me for taking action without his approval, then added, "The minute you stop doing that, I'll fire you." We were both exhausted by the strain of long hours.

Although caught in the middle and snarled at for doing my duty, I was strongly supported by two key people. Blake Budden of Section V, MI-6, wanted me to be a careful and courageous vetter. He was appalled that I had been understaffed at the start and at the dogged resistance of some OSS officers to my vetting their agents. One day he stomped over to Pearson's office and recommended that I be promoted immediately to major in order to fend off uncooperative majors and colonels. The British Army, Budden explained, often gave higher temporary rank when the job would benefit from it. He cited the case of a British captain who was to visit Marshal Tito, the Yugoslavian guerrilla leader in his mountain lair. The British made him a brigadier for that trip.

"No thanks," Pearson replied. "We don't do that." Civilians like Pearson were blind to the operational nightmare of low-ranking officers attempting to call the shots to higher-ups. My mother, ever a patient and wise counselor, reminded me that the quality of my work was more important than rank. However, Blake Budden's intervention and support was helpful. Pearson began to back me up more promptly and vigorously.

Meanwhile, Wilma Taber, my number-one secretary, became visibly concerned about the stress on me. A tall Nebraskan who wore her hair in a bun, she was exceptionally intelligent, forceful, and adept at office politics. She indicated a strong interest in my welfare, the full ramifications of which I didn't discover until November 1945 when she confessed she had been silently in love with me while I was dating another. Wilma was also grateful to me for having plucked her out of her job as a messenger girl to become my top assistant. Later, after being moved up to officer rank, she would say repeatedly, "You made my career." Wilma did all kinds of little things to make the job easier for me. She organized and motivated my other secretaries, coached me on how to handle long hours and frantic deadlines better, and even bravely volunteered to take messages to the hot-tempered Blake Budden when I was overwhelmed with work.

I can vividly remember those hectic six to eight weeks before the army crossed the Rhine in March. On the first of March I returned to my flat at 1:00 AM and collapsed. Army doctors, on hearing of my long hours, diagnosed exhaustion and ordered an emergency one-week medical leave. My leave was delayed for three weeks by the overriding priority of clearing agents to drop into Germany. The war demanded I continue until the crisis passed. Then I could go away for a rest.

OSS ordered me to take the medical leave on March 20, 1945, and the very next day I hopped onto the Cornish Riviera Express, which in eight hours wafted me 285 miles to Penzance on the English Channel.

By this time, the crunch of clearing spies to parachute into Germany had eased, and separating myself from the office proved easy. I boarded the train, lonely but relieved. Penzance surprised me from the start with its palm trees, cactus, and spring flowers. I stayed at the Queen's Hotel for a night and then in a cozy fisherman's house in Mousehole, just west of Penzance.

The army doctor was so right in sending me to Cornwall. It is a wild, romantic place with high cliffs, rugged hills, and snarling surf crashing against rocky beaches. I reveled in everything—the fresh air, the scenery, the history. Cornwall's remoteness explained why it had never been occupied by Saxons or Romans, although ancient Phoenicians visited it seeking tin, and it was shelled by the Spanish Armada in 1588.

The first forty-eight hours away completely rejuvenated me. I cycled twenty-five miles a day under a beating sun and steady wind, up and down abrupt hills beside the high coast. First, I went down to Land's End at the westernmost tip of England. I crossed the plateau some five hundred feet above sea level, every now and then whistling down into some dark glade where a granite farmhouse lay in the shadows of a dense copse. By clear brooks narcissi and daffodils grew wild. Up again I would struggle along the tortuous road to look briefly at the sea before soaring down again. On the cliff at Land's End, a fierce wind nearly blew me into the water. It was so marvelous to be free again, to run with the wind and not give a darn! From the high cliffs I watched great rollers smash against the rocks below and pile up in ravines or wash into the large caves.

The next day I biked over to St. Ives, a small fishing village on the north shore, approaching it on a five-hundred-foot cliff and then slicing diagonally down to the harbor. The water was light blue, almost as in the Caribbean, and the sand white.

Another day I went to sea with a fisherman from Mousehole. Passing closely along the coast, we sighted minesweepers, convoys, and the occasional oily splotch, mute testimony to an unfortunate ship. Little Belgian trawlers excited the commercial interest of their Cornish rivals. I asked my host to take me near the giant cliffs, but the sea was too rough. After nearly capsizing when the swell broke over the shallow ledge rock, we turned for home somewhat the wetter.

Many of the local fishermen had been at Dunkirk, the French port from which the battered British Army evacuated in May 1940. They led peaceful and quiet lives, fishing five evenings a week for five to nine hours.

Mrs. Simpson, my hostess, identified over fifty varieties of wild flowers that grew around Mousehole. She obtained bunches of daffodils for my return to London. Her husband pleased me to no end with an invitation to the local pub. We sat there for hours talking with sixty-year-old veterans of the sea and listening to the Belgian sailors speak Flemish.

I returned refreshed from medical leave in late March. My work hours became more civilized. And it cheered me to see spring erupt in that special glory caused by England's wet climate and knowledgeable gardeners. In the beginning of April everything burst into bloom: first, the crocuses and daffodils, then the tulips in brilliant black, red, yellow and purple, and clumps of rhododendron and azaleas. Along London's many tree-lined streets, clusters of yellow petals hung from the favored laburnum. After the drab London winter, the variety and richness of color lifted everyone's spirits. So did events across the channel, where the war against Germany was grinding to a close.

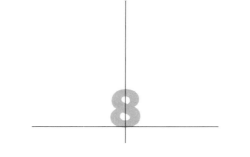

VICTORY IN EUROPE

In February 1945, all the world watched with baited breath as the Allies slogged toward the Rhine. We sensed that the winter lull with its dearth of Allied victories was about to end. It seemed like a year, instead of six months, since Patton had raced across France, liberating Paris and winging his way to the fortified Siegfried Line on Germany's western border. By March 7, the U.S. Ninth Army quickly seized a railway bridge at Remagen and crossed the Rhine between Bonn and Coblenz. On March 26, Americans captured Frankfurt-am-Main, and on April 1 British armies surrounded 300,000 German troops in the Ruhr. Eleven days later Roosevelt died at Warms Springs, Georgia, shocking the British as much as the Americans. His death inspired a delirious Hitler to proclaim that this was an omen: Like Frederick the Great's Prussia, his Third Reich would be saved at the last moment. The Allies were sad and wondered whether Harry Truman was up to the job. He was, but few sensed it then.

As Allied armies overran Germany, big questions remained. Would the Germans seek to form a redoubt in the Bavarian Alps? Where and when would Allied armies meet Soviet troops? At the time they were smashing through Poland, after a long, agonizing halt at Warsaw. Who would get to Berlin first?

The U.S. Ninth Army had reached the Elbe on April 11 and halted. Churchill, having a farsighted appreciation of Berlin's postwar significance, tried to persuade Eisenhower privately to march to Berlin. Such a move would have violated the Yalta agreement between the Soviet Union and the western Allies concerning the parts of Germany each victor would occupy, and Eisenhower declined, telling Churchill his mission was to defeat the German Army. The strongest remnant of that army, he believed, was then moving toward Czechoslovakia's mountains. Eisenhower did however overrun Saxony and Thuringia, a region near Czechoslovakia that had been earmarked for Soviet occupation. He postponed a withdrawal to the agreed line until OSS had recruited many top German rocket scientists, including Werner von Braun, for service in America's future rocket program.

The manner of recruitment was thrilling, at least for the Germans involved. Von Braun and many rocket scientists had fled their research headquarters at Peenemunde on the Baltic to avoid the Soviet Army, destroyed rocket facilities there, and sped toward the Ninth Army as it approached Weimar in Thuringia. OSS sought them out, just ahead of Soviet efforts to recruit or, if necessary, kidnap them. Both the United States and the Soviet Union had mounted ambitious intelligence operations to enlist the cream of German rocket scientists after the German collapse. OSS had launched Operation Paperclip to identify and capture German scientists working on the missile programs and to prevent them from falling into Soviet hands. A similar Soviet program, according to a knowledgeable CIA friend who served in OSS with me, appeared to have been better conceived and more effectively implemented than the American effort. The Soviet operation may have contributed to the early successes of Soviet space and missile projects in the 1950s.[1] A Soviet Sputnik orbited the earth in 1957 before the United States, with Von Braun's help, could duplicate and eventually surpass that Soviet achievement.

While Eisenhower's Ninth Army was snapping up rocket brainpower, Patton's Third Army overran the Dachau concentration camp near Munich. Immediately, newspapers around the world showed grisly pictures of emaciated Jewish survivors, little more than skeletons, peering out from behind barbed wire and stacks of dead inmates. The war could not end too soon. In London we watched and listened, helpless spectators. Heinrich Himmler, the number-two Nazi, tried to escape near Hamburg, was captured by the British, and then committed suicide. On April 30 Joseph Goebbels, Hitler's propaganda minister, swallowed cyanide, and later that day Hitler shot himself and his mistress, Eva Braun, in the desolate bunker below the chancellory in Berlin. The German armies surrendered on May 8, 1945, which became known as Victory in Europe, or V-E, Day.

The lights sprang on in London, revealing just how grubby the soot-covered city was, but no one cared. Crowds flocked to Trafalgar Square and Piccadilly Circus and surged down Pall Mall to see the king and queen appear on the balcony of Buckingham Palace, a short walking distance from our OSS offices. The staid English were ecstatic, jumping, screaming, slapping backs, kissing, and locating scarce whiskey to celebrate. The long war was over. No more boys would be maimed or killed in Europe. Hitler was dead.

After a rousing brunch, my friend Jane and I went off for a walk around the city. At 2 PM we joined thousands of others in front of Buckingham Palace for a glimpse of the king and queen. After taking a bus back to her flat to hear Churchill's address at 3 PM, we returned to town for a cocktail party at Norman Pearson's flat overlooking the trees of Green Park and the palace, which was brilliantly lit by antiaircraft floodlights. Big Ben glowed through the haze, and floodlights shot playfully around the sky. Hearing the roar of the crowd in front of the palace, our party set out to investigate. The king and queen appeared just as we arrived. Again, we traipsed down the mall, belting out our favorite national song, "America, the Beautiful." At the east end of the mall, the Edward VII gate was lit up. To the tune of "Roll out the Barrel," we snake-danced in a circle, then got going on Yale cheers, much to the mystification of the English.

Weaving into Trafalgar Square, we picked up some Canadians and their Welsh dates, who favored us with Welsh songs. Guys and gals climbed up on the lions to make speeches to the indifferent multitude. Occasional rockets shot off in Piccadilly. An American sailor joined us and did a combination of a jig and jitterbug to the tune of "Anchors Aweigh." The girls in their high heels were feeling the pavement by this time, and it being 2 AM, we decided to pile into Norman Pearson's car, which was supposedly parked nearby. Imagine our surprise upon discovering that it had been stolen during the festivities.

With victory in Europe, conversation at OSS quickly turned to new concerns. Would we be demobilized or shifted to the Pacific? Was there a determined German underground resistance? Would we need to track down top German intelligence and political leaders in order to nip any such effort in the bud? More and more of the staff were sent to the Continent, particularly to Paris. On May 9, Pearson told me I would be transferred to Germany in a month.

In early June, Pearson said I was to go to Wiesbaden near Frankfurt, where OSS-Germany was headquartered. The chief of the OSS mission was to be Allen Dulles, the most celebrated of all OSS spymasters in Europe. He had recently transferred from Bern, Switzerland, the scene of his great wartime successes. My assignment was challenging. On direct order from General Donovan, I was to vet all of Allen Dulles's wartime sources inside Germany, aptly named the "Crown Jewels." Pearson dryly reported to Washington, "Cutler was reassigned to our German station in relation to the final task of cleaning up the situation there."[2]

Pearson felt I had done a good job in cleaning up a messy situation in London. The chief of Section V, MI-6, wrote Pearson

Cutler has rendered very considerable help to us on all questions concerning the travel in and out of the UK of agents and persons in whom OSS was interested. Cutler has shown a complete understanding of the Home Office regulations and other technical details of this rather complex problem and his assistance has been invaluable.[3]

Col. James R. Forgan, the peacetime cohead of the Glore-Forgan investment bank and then chief of the OSS Detachment, European theater of operations, awarded me a certificate of merit for "brilliant initiative and conspicuous devotion to duty in a responsible position.[4] I was sad to be leaving London. It had been like a second home to me, and I had enjoyed my fine, spacious flat, good maid service, lovely parks, and friendly English people. Having long desired to go to Germany, I was nonetheless apprehensive about vetting SI spies there. On the one hand, jurisdictional rivalries, together with indecisiveness in high places, might put a swift end to my work. On the other, if my work continued, the difficulties of vetting wouldn't get started in earnest for several months. But I knew it was my duty to use all the means at my disposal to maintain an outwardly cheerful demeanor.

9

LIFE IN OCCUPIED GERMANY

THOSE OF US ON THE OSS STAFF WHO WERE BOUND FOR GERMANY left London on June 7, 1945, only thirty days after the German surrender. OSS, the U.S. Army, and the U.S. Army Air Force had to make do. The best available transportation was a Flying Fortress that had been hastily converted for civilian passengers. We flew very low, bouncing a lot. Across the English Channel the landscape revealed painful scars from six terrible years of war. As we flew over Calais we saw giant V-l sites carved out of wooded plots and badly marked up by bombs. France looked dead from the air—nothing on the roads, only three trains with steam up. Over Belgium and the Ardennes battlefront, we craned for views of the bloody Battle of the Bulge. Roads were clear and most towns untouched, save Bastogne. The worst visible damage lay across the German border, where small towns had been wiped out, mostly by artillery. The foxholes, mortar craters, and tank tracks were clearly visible. In some hamlets less than a quarter of the buildings remained standing.

The Fortress bounced onto steel matting the army had placed over bomb craters at the Wiesbaden airport, twenty-five miles west of Frankfurt-am-Main. We disembarked only to find that a second plane carrying our luggage had not left London, that no one expected us, and that the phones weren't working. Welcome to occupied Germany!

In the sweltering heat, we got a close look at how Allied bombing had treated an airport until recently operated by the *Luftwaffe*. Hangers bore bullet holes from low-flying attack bombers. Shattered fuselages of Messerschmitt 109s and Focke-Wulf 190s, the fighters that had sometimes struck fear into the hearts of Allied airmen, had been roughly shoved aside so that the airport could reopen. Eventually, we were loaded into army half-tracks and driven gingerly through the heavily bombed streets of Wiesbaden to the cobblestone-paved, sycamore-lined *allee* leading gently downhill and southward toward the Rhine. Our destination was the suburb of Biebrich, or Wiesbaden/Biebrich as the Germans called it.

Wiesbaden was a charming resort city. A spa since Roman times, it was blessed with a pleasant climate fostered by the Taunus Mountains, which shielded the city from cold northern winds. Wiesbaden was the capital of the state of Hesse from which the British had recruited Hessian mercenaries to fight against the colonies during the American Revolution. The war had badly damaged Wiesbaden, especially the luxury hotels built above the twenty-seven-foot-deep saline spas, but many elegant public buildings remained usable. Portions of the city had been smashed flat by a British raid in March 1945. In certain streets, people wove their way like slow-moving cows along trails through rubble piled several feet high. Some of the higher buildings had caved in, leaving behind heaps of brick, twisted steel, and rusted pipes. No one knew what lay underneath.

Wiesbaden, besides being a famous resort city, was a center of German champagne, or *sekt*, production. Conquering armies naturally pick the best sites for themselves. OSS chose the grandiose marble Henkel Truecken champagne factory. It was very modern, businesslike, and just the right size. Joachim von Ribbentrop, Hitler's long-time foreign minister, had started his career selling Henkel Truecken's green champagne, married the boss's daughter, and become independently wealthy. The factory's second story offered us needed offices, which we immediately occupied. Somehow OSS administrators had quickly requisitioned chairs, tables, and typewriters.

Part of the lower floor, where champagne had been produced, was transformed into our mess hall. We ate standing on an uncarpeted floor at long tables that normally sat sixteen. It was a big step down from London, where the Willow Run mess hall was no less than the dining room of the Grosvenor House Hotel, and the fact that we could drink unlimited quantities of green champagne didn't make up for the austere facilities. OSS served champagne free at the officers' club hastily opened in a confiscated building across the street. After a few weeks we tired of the green stuff and stopped drinking it. By then, enterprising quartermaster officers had discovered cognac, scotch, gin, and schnapps.

We were housed in an attractive Wagnerian subdivision across from the champagne factory. Streets bore operatic names like Ringstrasse and Niebelungenstrasse.

Living in the OSS compound at Wiesbaden/Biebrich was an unforgettable experience. We requisitioned for our use the finest facilities available. Our office building was modern and mostly undamaged. A former architect's spacious fourteen-room house served as residential quarters for twenty-two officers and we enjoyed the finest of German featherbeds. Two polite German spinsters served as housekeepers.

Still, we suffered many of the discomforts of our victims. British and American bombs had smashed Wiesbaden's utilities. For some sixty days, we had no heat and no hot water, and the drinking water was unsafe. Moreover, we were bored and without female companionship. The pretty OSS college graduates understandably responded to more attractive offers from high-ranking officers who had cars, took their dates to dinner at resort hotels, and offered other inducements such as riding on Hitler's yacht on the Rhine. I organized a bridge game to pass the idle hours and wrote home requesting a radio, magazines, and clippings from the *New York Times* about what was going on in Germany and the world.

By mid-July, conditions started to improve. OSS opened a tennis court in our compound, and on a quick trip to London my roommate, Charlie Stiassni, bought me a tennis racket at Harrod's for the princely sum of twenty-five dollars. An OSS officer and I began playing doubles with a couple of Germans, the mother and daughter who ran the officer's club.

By September, Gen. Omar Bradley's headquarters moved elsewhere, making Wiesbaden's tourist hotels and the fancy Opel swimming pool accessible to us at last. I was delighted to eat a few meals at small tables laid with tablecloths instead of at linoleum tables for sixteen.

When we arrived on June 7, 1945, Germany was in chaos, with its American occupiers slowly feeling their way in the midst of often-conflicting and vaguely defined objectives. The army proper faced two enormous tasks: deciding which troops to send to the Pacific for the continuing fight against Japan, and organizing a military government to provide law and order and restore destroyed public utility services. The army gave great credence to early reports that a German resistance might develop, aided by "werewolves"[1] who would, we were warned, stretch piano wire across streets at dusk to decapitate soldiers riding in jeeps. We were always squinting, looking for wires. Our attitude of distrust towards Germans was reinforced by the army's nonfraternization policy: Avoid all social contact with natives. For some weeks regulations required us to travel armed and with an escort after 7:00 PM. We were often out late, walking down to the Rhine or through German parks because the sun didn't set until late.

At the start of the American occupation, the three most common questions were, When will nonfraternization be lifted? When do we get hot water? And, especially for civilian OSS women, how in the heck do you keep from going out seven nights a week, and five times on Sunday? Soldiers came from forty miles away to barge into the girls' billets and demand dates. Colonels and generals lined up. Aspirants offered boat rides, plane rides, German camera film, champagne, and many other inducements.

The army quickly developed sensible exceptions to the nonfraternization policy. After requesting permission to resume German tutoring, discontinued during the heavy vetting job in London, I took frequent lessons from a German woman of French Huguenot descent. From her I learned that Herman Göring, the head of the *Luftwaffe*, had boasted early in the war that no British or American bombers would fly over Germany, or "my name is Mayer." When the bombers started flying over Wiesbaden regularly, Wiesbadeners mockingly named their flight path *Mayer Allee*. Many years later a Wiesbaden native told me that he had been thirteen years old when the British first attacked Wiesbaden with a thousand bombers. He was standing outside in the street when he heard a growing roar like an approaching freight train that went on and on, until finally the sky was swarming with bombers. He asked his father, a lieutenant general in the *Luftwaffe*, "Where are our fighters?" He replied, "The British destroyed the *Luftwaffe* over Britain." It was then that the boy knew Germany had lost the war.

Because of the nonfraternization policy, at first my contact with Germans was limited to my tutor and my tennis partners, the English-speaking wife of an imprisoned I. G. Farbenindustrie chemist who ran the officer's club and her pretty nineteen-year-old daughter who helped her. As for other Germans, it was as if we Americans floated by, twelve feet above the ground, gazing down at them as they silently went about their lives.

In London and even more in Wiesbaden, we relished hearing tales of Allen Dulles's success as America's outstanding spymaster in World War II. He enjoyed retelling accounts of his cases, interspersed with hearty laughter and dramatic gestures. All espionage tales are exciting, and his were especially so. They reflected the importance, glamour, and skill of our new espionage service. We were all starved for recognition, having been a hush-hush agency, and now with the war finished, we could tell of how "we" had outwitted the Germans, citing Allen Dulles's achievements as our own.

Allen Dulles and his brother, John Foster Dulles, the secretary of state under President Eisenhower, were sons of a Presbyterian minister. While John Foster Dulles was a man of very high principle—stiff and pompously Wilsonian—Allen was his opposite, a pragmatic, flexible, congenial, cultured, pipe-smoking squire who was passably fluent in German. Most important to his OSS work, he made many influential friends while serving for more than ten years in the State Department in Bern and Berlin. He was completely at home in European drawing rooms.

OSS sent Dulles to Bern, just over Germany's southern border, in October of 1942. Dulles achieved extraordinary success there, which experts attributed to three underlying factors. First, he was in the right place, the only neutral country on Germany's land border. Second, he was there at the right time, just when the tide of war turned against the Germans after Stalingrad, El Alamein, the American landings in North Africa and Sicily, and the decisive Soviet victory at Kursk.[2] All these major defeats happened by mid-1943, giving Germans a personal incentive to help the Allies bring down Hitler and preserve their own positions.

Third, Dulles took great risks that paid off. While the British schooled us that intelligence officers should be low profile, dealing with agents only through intermediaries, or "cutouts," Dulles quickly let out the word that he was American intelligence and left his light on, so to speak. He met directly with several top agents, which shocked MI-6. Germans hoping to help the West flocked to Dulles rather than to the hidden British agents in Switzerland. Among other critical secrets, Dulles learned through agents in Switzerland and Austria of the German atomic bomb program and obtained crude drawings of the V-l pilotless bomb and V-2 rocket that were to plague London in 1944.[3]

His most famous agent, the earlier-mentioned Fritz Kolbe, was a walk-on who volunteered, for no pay, to deliver top German secrets to Dulles in Bern. He had approached the British first, who turned him down because they thought him too good to be true and therefore that he was a German plant.[4] Too bad for the British, for his exploits became legendary.

Kolbe, whom we all knew as "Mr. Wood," had been the chief clerk of the German foreign office in Berlin and had access to all cables received from German ambassadors and military commands.[5] His job was to prepare daily summaries of cables for Foreign Minister Joachim von Ribbentrop, two doors away.

Kolbe delivered 1,600 German cables to Dulles, disclosing many top-level secrets. A German agent known as "Cicero" had regularly been transmitting to Berlin secret British documents in the possession of the British ambassador in Istanbul. Those documents included details of the methods Britain was using to persuade Turkey to join the war and, Norman Pearson believed, a sketchy outline of the planned Allied invasion of France. MI-6 assumed that Cicero pointed to an American leak until Pearson doggedly proved Kolbe's authenticity,[6] and President Roosevelt told Churchill that his embassy in Istanbul was compromised. The British eventually discovered that their ambassador's Albanian valet was rifling his safe.

The United States offered Kolbe American citizenship and a princely sum in gratitude for his services and because he would be a pariah in Germany if his role were ever revealed. After the war he lived for perhaps a year in New York City, lost his reward to a scam artist, then returned to Germany.

When Dulles first arrived in Bern in 1942, he had found entrée into the tiny group of eminent Germans courageously opposed to Hitler. He met Gero von Gaevernitz, the American son of a member of the German parliament, whom Dulles had known while working for the State Department in Berlin in the 1920s. Gaevernitz quickly became his principal contact with German friends in the loosely organized German opposition group known as the "Breakers." Ultimately, the Breakers included Adm. Wilhelm Canaris, head of the *Abwehr*, Gen. Ludwig Beck, a chief of the prewar German armed forces, and Carl Goerdeler, former longtime mayor of Leipzig. It was Gaevernitz who developed the Crown Jewels for Dulles, the top-notch network of some sixty members or affiliates of the Breakers. In the judgment of John Waller, author of a comprehensive masterpiece on World War II espionage, the Crown Jewels constituted a nucleus of leaders deemed acceptable in a postwar Germany.[7]

In early April 1944 Dulles telegraphed Donovan saying that the Breakers were ready to attempt a coup and eliminate Hitler. He asked Donovan for directions.[8] Donovan reputedly reported to Roosevelt personally that a plot to kill Hitler was building, to which Roosevelt, according to Donovan's deputy, replied, "If we assist in an effort to kill him, the enemy might attempt to kill me."[9] Donovan then instructed Dulles not to aid the conspirators in their plot, which took place on July 20 and failed. Most of the Crown Jewels were implicated in the plot and had to flee the Gestapo. Many were executed, including Admiral Canaris, whose sacrifice led Donovan and Dulles to befriend Frau Canaris after the surrender.

In 1945, those of us in Wiesbaden were proud of all the then-known accomplishments of the Crown Jewels. Because of Allen Dulles's masterful uncovering of German secrets through Kolbe and the Crown Jewels, for years thereafter the United States rated the significance of human intelligence very highly.[10]

I had more on my mind than marveling at Allen Dulles and his stories. When Norman Pearson told me in May 1945 that OSS would send me to Wiesbaden, he explained, rather cursorily, "You are to clean up the situation there." Indeed, there was much confusion at my new quarters. In addition to offices being constructed within a former champagne factory, missions were unclear and changing. SI, which wanted to repatriate and perhaps discharge agents who had served during the final days of the war, also pondered whether to continue espionage directed at identifying the intentions of Germany's potential leaders. X-2 continued to search vigorously for German intelligence's top personnel to be sure they were neutralized and to interrogate leaders like General Ernst Kaltenbrunner, who had succeeded Himmler as the head of the SS in May after the latter's suicide. Earlier Kaltenbrunner had served as the powerful and notorious head of the Headquarters for State Security (*Reichssicherheitshauptamt*), a position that later earned him a conviction at the Nuremberg war crimes tribunal. OSS interrogated him for several reasons, not least to find out what had happened to American spies captured by German intelligence and to learn if German intelligence had left agent networks behind the Soviet armies in Eastern Europe (they had) that might cooperate with the Americans against the Russians (one did). For example, in the office next to mine, my friend Jane, who was fluent in German, extracted the names and backgrounds of key German intelligence officers from a lengthy transcript of the Kaltenbrunner interrogation.

My own job at Wiesbaden was to vet the forty-odd agents of X-2 and SI, plus an additional forty to eighty cutouts and informants.[11] In addition, Colonel Suhling, head of the mission, asked me to vet all of Allen Dulles's surviving Crown Jewels.[12] My reports to Washington indicated that SI and X-2 cooperated in permitting their agents to be vetted by a stranger to their operations. Perhaps the increased cooperation reflected high-level oversight and encouragement not directly known to me. Often in my vetting assignment, I was a pawn in a conflict between X-2 and SI higher-ups over the "security of OSS" versus the "independence of SI."

Gero von Gaevernitz, Dulles's able factotum, held biographies of the sixty Crown Jewels that he refused to turn over to me until Allen Dulles, on request from Major General Donovan in Washington, directly intervened.[13] I used the X-2 forms I had developed for Europewide use and wirelessed names back to Wilma Taber, my successor in London, for her to check against the British registry of 1.5 million "names" of persons either friendly or hostile. I was fascinated to read the dramatic data on the Crown Jewels. As noted, they were not spies in the ordinary sense, but rather well-placed dissenters within the German establishment—the church, the aristocracy, the army, and political circles. Those members of the Breakers conspiracy who had not been executed and survived thought of themselves as "white" German advisors to the Americans, in contrast to Communist "reds" and Nazi "browns" (they wore brown shirts). After Hitler's demise, however, a majority of the Crown Jewels wished for no further role in espionage or work with foreigners. For example, Hans Bernd Gisevius, the principal contact between the German Resistance and Dulles, "never claimed to be an American agent or wanted to be considered one. He was a member of the Resistance *in liaison* with the Americans."[14]

Other Crown Jewels were willing to carry on, especially those who shared OSS's rapidly rising curiosity and apprehension about what the Soviet military government was up to in Germany. The Soviets had been looting German factories for reparations and printing counterfeit marks to support the Soviet Army. The Russians were understandably vindictive toward a country that had killed twenty-seven million of their fellow citizens, and many Crown Jewels were apprehensive about the pendulum of revenge swinging too far against their fatherland.

I interviewed Gaevernitz, found him charming and superficially cooperative. A review of CIA files in 1989 by historian Tim Naftali led him to conclude that Gaevernitz successfully withheld the biographies from me until my assignment officially ended in early January 1946. I don't recall whether I saw the biographies or not, for vetting after the war was both less vital and less hectic than in London, and therefore less memorable. At least once I went into the field, to Paris, to interrogate people about the purported record of a former *Abwehr* officer who had served there, but I spent most of that visit sightseeing, not vetting.

As summer progressed, X-2 vetting became even more routine. At first we worked seven days a week, then six days, then five and a half days. Each month, vetting seemed increasingly less vital than other matters. All of us became engrossed in watching history unfold. From the sidelines we read about the last summit meeting of the wartime Allies at Potsdam in July and watched the occupation army's struggle to fill the huge vacuum created by the total disappearance of a central German government. Meanwhile, swirling around us was the great commotion of transferring soldiers, first to the Pacific to fight Japan, and then, after the Japanese surrender on August 15, back home to the United States.

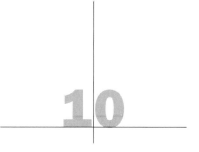

AMERICA'S CHALLENGE
IN GERMANY

GOVERNING A TOTALLY DEFEATED GERMANY POSED NEW CHAL-
lenges to the conquering Allies, especially to the Americans. The Russians,
French, and British harbored a more intense hatred of the Germans than
the Americans, who mixed hatred, paradoxically, with a quickly displayed
desire to be liked and admired by our former enemies, no matter what.
Little time passed before the Russians, so popular with us in the flush of
victory when our armies met in April at the Elbe a hundred miles west of
Berlin, began showing their virulent nationalist paranoia. Stalin believed
—and all Russians trembled under his tyrannical thumb—that the western Allies were plotting against the Soviet Union, and to combat them he
mounted a campaign of deception and set about sabotaging agreements
made with his allies.

At Yalta in February, Stalin, Churchill, and Roosevelt had agreed that
in occupying Germany, each of their armies would be assigned a particular geographic zone to administer. In Wiesbaden, we spectators joked
about the division of Germany into zones of occupation: the Russians got
the agriculture (Prussia); the British, the industry and coal (the Ruhr);
and the Americans, the scenery (Bavaria and the Alps).[1]

At a London conference of foreign ministers, the Allies had also agreed
that Hitler's capital, Berlin, would be jointly occupied by the Soviet
Union, Britain, France, and the United States. However, the Soviets, who
had conquered Berlin in early May, prevented the western Allies from
entering Berlin until July, which is when Allen Dulles went there to open
an OSS office. Even then the Soviets restricted access, as I recall, to one
highway, one canal, and two railroads—an ominous portent of what was

to come in 1948 when they cut off all ground access and the historically famous American-British Berlin airlift broke the blockade.

In the immediate aftermath of war, the U.S. Army had to shift gears from the familiar role of fighting to the new one of occupying a foreign land and helping supervise the defeated enemy's efforts to restore a shattered economy. How to do this? There was no central government left. Nor did anyone propose that one be recreated. The Allies agreed that the German government should be decentralized, reversing the trend toward consolidating power in Berlin under Bismarck, the kaiser, and Hitler. Hereafter, decisions would be made at the state or municipal level.

Immediately, the question arose, could we trust state and municipal employees to do right if they consisted largely of former Nazis, as we suspected? The answer, we Americans thought, was to weed the Nazis out of both local government and the German staff hired to assist us in overseeing that government. We would create a questionnaire—a *Fragenbogen*—delving into each employee's social, governmental, and political experience and past affiliations. An exhaustive document developed by the CIC duly appeared; it elicited vast amounts of information about the subject, down to prior membership in the *Hitler Jugend*, or Hitler Youth. Anyone who had belonged to a Nazi organization would be barred from government work—or so we thought.

That fall the high-spirited Gen. George S. Patton vented his anger at this somewhat impractical denazification policy. Most Germans, after all, had been affiliated with the Nazis in some fashion. Patton's Third Army governed Bavaria and the southern part of Germany. He gave high priority to restoring disrupted utilities and, apparently, knowingly permitted some Nazi functionaries to resume utility jobs they had previously held. The American press inquired if he had hired Nazis. Ever blunt, Patton replied that when it came to sewer engineers, the difference between Nazis and other Germans was no greater than the difference between Republicans and Democrats at home; the job had to be done by those who could do it best.

His remarks could not have been more ill advised. They created an instant furor back home. Two years earlier in Sicily, General Eisenhower had stoutly resisted an emotional press campaign for him to relieve the impetuous general after he slapped a hospitalized soldier for supposed malingering. This was the last straw. Eisenhower summarily removed Patton from his treasured command of the prestigious Third Army, transferring him to the obscure Fifteenth Army charged with writing the history of the war. In early December Patton was killed in a car crash at Mannheim.

Though insensitive and colorfully outspoken, Patton was correct in attaching high priority to the restoration of electricity, telephones, clean water, and trolleys. We cared more about restoring Germany's damaged coal mines and transportation system than about the unemployment rate, which increased as emaciated German prisoners returned home. Personally, I felt that if we didn't succeed in avoiding famine and intense suffering from the cold of the pending winter, there would be trouble.

The Allied military government and local authorities worked long and hard to tease some semblance of order out of sheer chaos, but the results were spotty. Some cities—like Frankfurt, where Eisenhower was stationed, and Hamburg in the British zone—restored trolley service much sooner than others. Much depended on the ability of local military officials. In many locations military government simply broke down.

Another, longer-term problem was determining how to reeducate the Germans so that they would stop waging wars of aggression and uncritically following chauvinistic leaders on white horses. Hitlerite textbooks would have to be replaced in the schools, and somehow the Germans would have to come to learn the value of democracy. Some Americans fretted over the bland German press, which seemed to glory in being totally apolitical and uncritical. Should prodemocracy news be spoon-fed to the local newspapers? Should we occupiers sponsor a radio station?

Germany was so shattered, the United States so powerful. I felt that we American occupiers were on trial as representatives of democracy. Incidentally, General Eisenhower stated that the success of the Allied occupation of Germany would be determined if, fifty years later, Germany was democratic, peaceful, and strong.[2] History proved the prescience of this statement, but at the time it wasn't encouraging to witness the immaturity of the average American soldier. Forget the problems of the occupation—he just wanted to drive his jeep faster and go home.

As to reeducating the Germans, Americans struck me as inexcusably inept. No doubt I expected too much, being only twenty-eight and accustomed to the efficiency of elite units like B-29 bomber wings and OSS, but it bothered me enough to complain to my hometown newspaper:

> You get discouraged because you believe that the job is being fumbled badly, that there is no hope of immediate improvement, that all channels for constructive criticism are blocked off, that the leaders at the top just do not know how bad things are.

You feel that the military government is understaffed, that, not having top priorities on personnel, they were not able to recruit the able administrators and linguists needed for the toughest assignment before them.

The best thing for the United States . . . would be for the military government to be made civilian, with high salaries and five-year contracts, to have the Army become a police force. Then maybe the public safety officer would turn out to be an experienced police officer from an American city and not a former veterinarian and a poor one at that.[3]

My boss back at the law firm in New York read my intemperate editorial and quickly responded with a force only slightly moderated by tact:

Like all your letters it is very interesting, but you were being a little bit too outspoken and frank for your own good with respect to the military government of Germany. Why not wait until you are out of uniform? . . . I have no doubt our numerous correspondents in Germany (with anonymous help from far-seeing and patriotic citizens like yourself) will soon lay the facts before the public.[4]

On August 6, 1945, only three months after Germany's surrender, the United States dropped the first atomic bomb on Hiroshima, followed three days later by a second on Nagasaki, seeking to compel a Japanese surrender and avert the dreaded heavy loss of American lives in the already planned invasion of Japan. The Pacific war ended with Japan's surrender on August 15. For a short time, the United States stood as the sole nuclear power and clearly the mightiest military force in the world. We didn't know then that Klaus Fuchs, a German-born British citizen who was also a Soviet spy, had filched the design for the American atomic bomb from his colleagues at Los Alamos and given it to the Soviet Union.

Even though OSS became increasingly concerned over mounting evidence of Soviet hostility toward the West, the United States rapidly wound down its worldwide military effort in the wake of Japan's capitulation. There was a rush for troops to go home and budgets to be slashed, and OSS, unknown to us in Germany, was unsuccessfully fighting for its life. In late September President Harry Truman formally disbanded OSS. The reasons were complex. A year earlier in October 1944 Roosevelt had asked Donovan to outline a foreign intelligence service to be created after the war. Donovan quickly drafted a proposal for a service reporting directly to the president rather than to some cabinet officer. Immediately, opponents sought to water down the proposal, particularly by specifying that the new service report to an existing department, usually their own. When Roosevelt died in April 1945, OSS lost its best friend. Opponents competed for the new president's ear, and Donovan was virtually shut out. In the end, they won. Truman disbanded OSS on October 1, 1945.

Why OSS was disbanded is a long story, one definitively researched and recorded by Thomas F. Troy in *Donovan and the CIA*.[5] Two major factors were the relentless opposition of the military intelligence services, especially G-2, and J. Edgar Hoover, the tyrannical, feisty, duplicitous long-time head of the FBI. Hoover used lackey journalists like Drew Pearson and the gossip columnist Walter Winchell to attack OSS at every turn and thereby cool Congress and Truman toward it. In any event, the new president was all too easily convinced (until he reversed his position in mid-1947) that the United States did not need a permanent foreign secret service. Perhaps Hoover coveted that role for his agency; whatever his motives, he wanted to deny it to his bitter rival.

On October 1, 1945, Truman split OSS into two sections. One, consisting of the old X-2 and SI, was renamed the Strategic Services Unit (SSU) and assigned to the War Department. SSU didn't report to the Joint Chiefs of Staff as OSS had. The second section, Research and Analysis (R&A), which some historians believe was the most productive of the old OSS branches, was transferred to, or literally dumped on, a woefully unprepared State Department. In Germany, as OSS morphed into SSU, we scarcely noticed the difference, except for budget cuts. Although our personnel dwindled, a hard core of professionals remained, many of whom would rise high in the CIA that Truman and Congress created in July 1947 after the Soviet Union's tanks crushed Czechoslovakia.

When Truman terminated OSS Donovan promptly became deputy director of the American prosecution team at the war crimes trial of the twenty-four top Nazi leaders, which was to start in Nuremberg on October 18, 1945. Hitler hadn't converted Germany into a megamonster all by his lonesome. He had been ably assisted by other Nazi leaders, primarily Joseph Goebbels, the brilliant propagandist who skillfully manipulated the hearts and minds of Germans; Heinrich Himmler, the shrewd, cold-blooded, but able, chief of the elite SS and the dreaded Gestapo; and Herman Göring, the fat, flamboyant leader of the *Luftwaffe* whose initial successes had given way to a series of defeats, starting with the Battle of Britain in 1940, that ultimately cost him the führer's favor.

Watching history unfold from the sidelines in Wiesbaden, I had to wonder what manner of people these Germans were, these people who had enthusiastically supported Hitler and risen from the ashes of World War I to smash France and overrun Europe. When Norman Pearson let me choose between serving in France or Germany, I had opted for the latter, quickly throwing away the advantages of six years' study of French, primarily because I wanted to answer this question. In my bones I felt that the Germans, with their raw industrial power and thirst for leadership, would once again rise to economic and political significance. Secretary of Treasury Henry Morgenthau's plan for crippling Germany by converting it to pasture land smacked of the Romans destroying Carthage by salting its earth and was not likely to happen.

And so, during the summer, along with many other Americans in Wiesbaden, we at OSS became people watchers. There being no public transport, Germans traveled on foot, bicycle, and the occasional horse cart. The more prosperous Germans looked healthy and well dressed. Some men sported Tyrolean hats; a few wore attractive knickers and long wool stockings. The peasants from the countryside had a timeless, ruddy, weather-beaten look as they jogged along the street in their black clothes. Some older women wore skirts to their ankles. Every German carried a small bundle, some no doubt because they were moving home, others because they were foraging for food. *Wehrmacht* men returned home in clean, but unpressed, uniforms from which the insignia had been torn off, and many were burned almost black from the sun. They stared at me with beady eyes, whether with a permanent squint from too much sun or a look of hate, I couldn't tell. Civilians, by contrast, stared straight ahead when they spotted me. There were no Fräuleins flirting with Americans.

One day when I was out in the country, two children tagged along after me to point out the air raid shelters, brick kilns, and Russian slave labor camps. I tried to talk to them, but my limited German couldn't handle the Hessian dialect.

I lived within a mile of the Rhine. One day I crossed the broad river to the French zone, where the occupying soldiers were marching hundreds of bedraggled German prisoners from the dreaded *Waffen SS*. Some had dropped flat in the road, and two or three looked dead. The survivors had apparently endured a long march from a prison camp, presumably to a new prison camp, and I had heard that their French captors had treated them harshly. Most U.S. infantrymen felt that such treatment was justified because the SS had massacred American prisoners at Malmedy in early 1945. I didn't agree. The brutal French treatment shocked me, and after saying so to a heavily decorated American soldier, I got a sharp retort. "Listen, Lieutenant, have you ever seen any of the prisoner of war camps we liberated?" That ended that.

Later at Limburg, north of Wiesbaden, I spotted no outward signs of war. Germans rode horses, worked over the wheat-cocks, carried water to the cattle trough, and placed washing on the bank to dry. In the forests, though, I glimpsed a harbinger of winter. Endless lines of women and old men pushed carts—some big enough to be pulled by horses—loaded with green wood, twigs, brambles, anything that might burn. When a cart broke down, other carts flowed around it like logs swirling by a rock in a river. Our jeep, driven by a soldier who delighted in honking madly at the old peasant women, screamed through the logjam, driving the procession over on the road's shoulder. Each cart trip couldn't have produced enough wood for more than a single meal. We more fortunate Americans had coal.

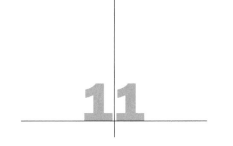

GERMAN EVASIVENESS
ABOUT HITLER

WATCHING GERMANS, WHILE FASCINATING, DIDN'T TELL ME WHAT they were thinking. Although nonfraternization rules at first prohibited us from talking to Germans, their were exceptions to the rules—we could talk to servants and language tutors. I quickly seized this opportunity to find out more about the Germans, to crack the mystery of why they had so slavishly supported Hitler and how they felt about his aggressive wars and disastrous defeat. When questioned directly, most claimed never to have been Nazis, and never to have been associated with them. Only casual conversation and indirect questions—my legal training had taught me to deal this way with reluctant witnesses—exposed their Nazi sympathies. For example, my German tutor explained the motive behind the war by spouting Goebbels's line that populous Germany needed *Lebensraum*, meaning land or living space outside the homeland.

The two English-speaking spinsters who worked as housekeepers in the officers' billet where I lived claimed to have English relatives. Though polite and proper, like most Germans in Wiesbaden they showed no basic concept of right or wrong when I asked them why they had lost the war. War mistakes were merely strategic errors: "If only Hitler had stopped in the Ukraine—we needed the corn and wheat. Why did he go on and on and on? Hitler was a fool to attack the United States. You had so much material, thousands and thousands of planes. Our soldiers were so brave, they had so little to eat, they fought so well."

Later I would hear additional strained explanations of why the Germans had lost the war:

"He made such a big mistake. He shouldn't have gone beyond the Don in Russia."

"If only America hadn't attacked us." (In fact, Hitler declared war on the United States four days after Pearl Harbor.)
"America had too many planes for the *Terrorangriffe* [terror attacks]."
"The German Army wasn't beaten, it just lacked matériel."
Senior *Wehrmacht* officers expressed a similar lack of guilt. They told American and British interrogators from the joint intelligence committee of SHAEF,

> Success is right. What does not succeed is wrong. It was, for example, wrong to persecute the Jews before the war since that set the Anglo-Americans against Germany. It would have been right to postpone the anti-Jewish campaign and begin it after Germany had won the war. It was wrong to bomb England in 1940. If they had refrained, Great Britain would have joined Hitler in the war against Russia. It was wrong to treat Russian and Polish [prisoners of war] like cattle since they will treat Germans in the same way. It was wrong to declare war against the USA and Russia because they are together stronger than Germany.[1]

No German ever mentioned to me the possibility that the war resulted from a clash of principles, or that the Allies' strength in matériel may have been the inevitable result of Germany having alienated world opinion by attacking many innocent nations.

For a short time after their defeat, a number of Germans simply could not accept the fact that Hitler had died, even though his own government had reported his death and proclaimed navy Adm. Karl Dönitz as his successor. The führer's body had not been found, and rumors persisted that he was still alive.[2] At a U.S. Army–organized "New England town forum" in Wiesbaden to which fifty "white Germans" were invited, the first question asked was whether the Allies really believed Hitler was dead. A German-speaking lieutenant answered, "It doesn't matter. The important thing is that the Hitler idea is dead." But it did matter. A few Germans told me that some of their compatriots couldn't lay their pan-Germanism to rest until they knew Hitler was truly dead.

This selected audience did also ask whether all Germans were blamed for the concentration camp at Buchenwald. That was the million-dollar question. While many Germans expressed remorse about the camps, they almost universally denied ever being aware of the secret extermination of Jews at places like Auschwitz in Poland and Buchenwald in their own backyard. Those who admitted to having heard of the camps made the argument that they had simply housed undesirables—Jews, homosexuals, and gypsies.

How much a handful of Germans actually did know I learned from a surviving Jewish Dachau concentration camp prisoner who later moved to Canada. He was being used as a slave laborer to build an underground aircraft factory in the Alps. One day, dressed in a telltale striped prison uniform and gaunt from near starvation, he was trekking slowly across a hill to work when he passed a German mother and her small son picking berries. She whispered to the son, "There's a Jew from the camp; woe unto us if the world finds out what we have done to them!"

Despite this story, I generally believed Germans when they professed limited knowledge of the camps. I told them, however, that the German people were responsible for extinguishing their ability to know by acquiescing to Hitler's destruction of free speech and opposition political parties; they didn't agree. When I tried to spell out that a free press and political opposition parties would have exposed and put an end to the concentration camps, they would gaze at me, puzzled. The truth was, Germans couldn't conceive of challenging authority. They had a saying: *Alles kommt von oben,* or everything comes from the top. Those few who did concede my point couldn't let it rest there. They immediately countered with a question of their own: how then could the United States be an ally of Stalin's Russia?

Once I had a rare opportunity to plumb the German mind when I spent four hours talking with Dr. Neugebauer, the man who had once worked as a chemist at I. G. Farbenindustrie in Frankfurt. The U.S. Army had briefly imprisoned him on a suspicion, later discounted, that he might have been involved in his company's supplying gas to kill Jews more quickly and economically in the concentration camps. I pressed Dr. Neugebauer again and again about what German intellectuals were thinking when they let Hitler rise to power. It was a combination, he told me, of Hitler's wild popularity and the greatest German weakness—a heritage of doing whatever one was told to do. There was a German word for this that was even more illuminating than the saying *Alles kommt von oben,* and that was *Kadavergehersamm,* which literally meant obedience until death. Military commanders had relied on *Kadavergehersamm* to ensure that soldiers faithfully carried out even the most controversial orders.

I asked Dr. Neugebauer how the Germans would remember Hitler in the future. As "the man who ruined Germany," he replied. When I turned the conversation to Buchenwald, he just looked sick. Whether he was ashamed or realized the Allies were blaming all Germans for the atrocity of the Holocaust, I couldn't fathom.

We also talked about the future of Germany. He was one of the few politically astute Germans I met. He advised that the United States keep a large army in Europe, which was remarkably prescient. (The North Atlantic Treaty Organization was later created, as the saying went, to keep the Americans in Europe, the Germans down, and the Russians out.) "What should be done with the younger generation educated under the Nazis?" I asked. He replied, "Don't you think we older Germans have thought about that? Some of them will be reeducated. Others never completely came under Nazi sway. My youngest daughter is an example of that. By feigning sickness she managed to stay out of the German Army. She now openly wants to emigrate to America."

In early July, with the vetting work increasingly dull to me and annoying to others—I was regarded as a redundant double-check on the operating officers' judgment—I began to consider the possibility of changing jobs. There was a big catch. Donovan wanted the vetting done, and I had been picked by the brass to do it. I could be reassigned only if someone with substantial power requested me to do a job for him. There was no thought of going home. My military service had been too short to warrant discharge even after the Japanese surrendered in mid-August. The army's system for discharging soldiers properly gave priority to those who had served the longest, and I had only two and a half years of military service (seven months of civilian work with the Board of Economic Warfare didn't count). I expected to be in Europe for another year.

In September the State Department offered me a position in Berlin on the condition I sign a one-year contract, but there was no assurance that the military would release me. A better idea popped into my head. Maybe I could persuade OSS to transfer me to Berlin. A vivacious Women's Army Corp (WAC) captain, Betty Harding, whom I had met in Washington while working for the Board of Economic Warfare, had returned to Wiesbaden from temporary duty at OSS-Berlin. Her stories of derring-do there made it sound much more exciting than our stale, hermit-like life in the Wiesbaden garrison.

My benevolent X-2 chief, Andrew Berding, had been replaced by a tough new successor, Crosby Lewis. If I could convince Lewis that my vetting job was nearly done, and if there was an OSS manpower shortage in Berlin, he might assign me there. I put it to him directly, adding that long ago I had been recruited for field duty with SCI teams and would like to do similar work with American agents in Berlin. I had been taking German lessons at my own expense and was ready to go. After talking with Berlin and arranging to bring a colleague from London to replace me as vetting officer, he agreed.

And so on September 22, I boarded an OSS plane at Wiesbaden loaded with an assorted cargo of odd characters, including an agent too fat for his seat belt. We zoomed down the recently rebuilt, concrete runway and took off for an easy flight to Berlin. After dozing off for lack of sleep the night before, I awakened to glimpse the rolling Thuringian forests and the Elbe River in the flat plain west of Potsdam, where our Ninth and First armies had met the Soviet armies five months earlier.

Berlin's dangerous espionage cases and active social life immediately erased the doldrums I'd experienced in Wiesbaden. The nonfraternization policy had already ended, which allowed me to pursue social contacts with a number of non-nationalistic Germans I met in Berlin. In September I began recruiting and supervising many agents who were college educated, well traveled, and more politically sophisticated than their compatriots. Most had served in the elite *Abwehr* intelligence service, 10 percent of whose members had sympathized with the plot to assassinate Hitler in July of 1944.[3]

Berliners, unlike their country cousins in Wiesbaden, were typical big-city sophisticates. They resembled New Yorkers—a diverse group of energetic fast talkers with a dry wit. I spent many evenings with Barbara Güttler and her dignified Silesian mother. Barbara had been secretary to the chief of the *Abwehr* in German-occupied Paris and, in fact, had been jailed for a day when her boss was temporarily implicated in the failed July 1944 putsch against Hitler. Mother and daughter spoke several languages, including nearly perfect English, and had traveled extensively abroad. Barbara had seen *Life* magazine photographs of emaciated Jewish prisoners at Buchenwald, and her mother had heard a person say that some prisoners at Dachau were run around the yard until they died of exhaustion. Germans, they told me, wouldn't believe a new fact such as the atrocities that had been committed inside concentration camps, unless it was repeated eight or more times. I commented that all Germans should be shown newsreels of the dead and starving inmates in the concentration camps, and they agreed.

Few Berliners were so reasonable. A faint justification for anti-Semitism came from a Berliner who had been a state prosecutor before the war. He said that it stemmed in part from the fact that Jews studied harder than others and gained admission to the finest universities and medical schools at a rate markedly disproportionate to their population, which was less than 4 percent of Berlin's population. He failed to mention that Jews were excluded from pursuing careers in the civil service, agriculture, and many businesses.

Even comparatively sophisticated Berliners tended to be politically naive, or worse, just plain blank. Like other Germans, and very much unlike the skeptical French, they believed everything their leaders told them. After years of being fed propaganda about the supposed superiority of the Aryan race and becoming intoxicated by Germany's many victories in the first four years of the war, they were confused and bitter about their humiliating defeat and hadn't begun to sort out fact from fiction. One ex-*Luftwaffe* officer I met, a German Rhodes scholar no less, echoed Hitler's line that the world had unjustly opposed Germany's annexation of Austria. After all, he said, Germany and Austria had always been one country. His argument totally ignored the wars that had been fought between Bismarck's Prussia, the originator of modern Germany, and its archrival, Austria.

At first the vast majority of Berliners complained bitterly about the Soviets raping and looting their way through Berlin following Hitler's demise. Why, they wanted to know, had the U.S. Army stopped at the Elbe River one hundred miles west of Berlin instead of marching into the city ahead of the Russians? Later, these same Germans became very critical of the Allies for not feeding them. I told them that Europe as a whole was suffering food and coal shortages, not just Germany, something they found hard to believe. They didn't realize the destruction their country had wrought on the world and the hatred they had stirred up.

I could only put my hope in the younger generation of Germans who hadn't been responsible for bringing Hitler to power. The older generation was politically immature and hypernationalistic, and American efforts to educate them, such as publishing a daily newspaper and monthly magazine, opening radio stations, bringing émigré faculty back to universities, and later publicizing the Nuremberg war crimes trial, were too sporadic and mild. I thought we needed an aggressive office of war information staffed by persons with a flare for American propaganda.[4] Truman had killed that idea.

Not unexpectedly, many Berliners falsely claimed to have been victims of fascism and even fooled some American officers into casually accepting their lies. One day I was asked to inspect some homes with an eye toward requisitioning them for American officers. The first owner I encountered produced an apparently genuine letter from an American colonel certifying that he was a Victim of Fascism, and that his house should not be requisitioned. A second owner explained that the Americans had already requisitioned his other house, then showed me a letter with some American colonel's letterhead saying this house was not to be touched. The letter was merely signed with the initials of the colonel's German secretary; at any rate, the colonel had no authority to grant the exemption. I went back to the first apparently genuine victim and asked him for names of Nazi bigwigs whose homes we might requisition. He came up with someone who had joined the Nazi party in 1932, before Hitler came to power, but this man too produced an exemption letter from an unauthorized American officer. Nevertheless, the requisition took place.

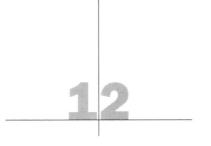

WAR-TORN CONTINENT
AND BERLIN

BEFORE MOVING TO BERLIN—INDEED, ALMOST IMMEDIATELY after settling in at Wiesbaden—I started touring the war-ravaged German countryside on weekends. I rode the OSS tour truck with up to a dozen others, hitchhiked, and occasionally obtained a jeep from the motor pool.

The German countryside around Wiesbaden was distinctly different from America's rural areas. American farmers build their homes and barns on their land. In central and northern Germany, all farmhouses cluster together in the central village, or *dorf*, and each morning farmers walk out from the village to work their plots. A countryside without houses and barns yields spectacular vistas. We would bound up and down the hills near the Rhine, swooping into quiet villages with orange-tile roofs. On the road to Bonn in July we drove across the Taunus mountains with its ridges overlooking miles of sharply broken terrain—fields here, forests there, and occasionally a Rhine castle atop some sugarloaf. In late August I traveled south to Bavaria. There, farmers built their homes directly over their barns so that the cows' heat would help warm the house. Apparently, Bavarians were oblivious to the odor of manure.

One Sunday six of us picnicked in the forest near Wiesbaden, full of Scotch pine, spruce, beach, birch, and fields of brilliant purple foxgloves. We stumbled on an SS ambulance convoy that had been abandoned and then looted, but there were still helmets and other German equipment, and a letter, nine months' old, from Göring exhorting German troops to carry on.

The countryside to the east, between Wiesbaden and Frankfurt, was flat with fields of ripened wheat. To the south lay the Main River, which meandered through industrial towns to meet the Rhine at Mainz. From a few miles away these towns seemed untouched and preindustrial. Then a crossing autobahn or high-tension power line abruptly reminded us of the more recent German state.

Once my assistant, Anne Heyneger, Jane, and I drove south to Heidelberg for a picnic at fifty miles an hour along Hitler's autobahn, which shot south from Frankfurt in a monotonous straight line. We scampered off it near Heidelberg, leaving industrialized Nazi Germany for the curving roads of yesteryear, with their half-timbered sixteenth-century homes, crops of wheat and barley, and limestone quarries. The university town of Heidelberg was untouched, save for the usual blown bridges. As the three of us stood on a parapet looking down on the city far below, a Black Widow night-fighter flashed down the narrow Neckar River valley, hopping over the shattered bridges as lightly as a thistle bumping along the ground, then went into a steep climb high above the city. Germans' heads turned quickly for planes. Americans were glad to have the air force putting in an appearance now and then, lest the conquered get any ideas about rising from their ashes.

Most enjoyable were our weekend excursions along the Rhine, which was scenic despite all the collapsed bridges. We traveled to Coblenz and Bonn, as well as Cologne in the British zone, some 125 miles northwest of Wiesbaden. To get to Coblenz, where the Moselle flows into the Rhine from France and Luxembourg, we passed vineyards hugging steep slopes and castles atop the bluffs. Upon reaching our destination we saw unique reminders of the recent bitter fighting. Walls bore frantic German slogans: *Für die Freiheit unseres Volkes* (for our people's freedom), *Für den Sieg* (for victory), *Coblenz bleibt treu* (Coblenz remains loyal). I also saw, scribbled during the heat of battle *Wir Kapitulieren* (we surrender).

At Cologne, the tallest cathedral in Germany had miraculously avoided destruction when a thousand British night-bombers devastated the city. It was in retaliation for this that Germany had demolished England's Coventry, also a cathedral town. Allied soldiers took great pride in having spared the Cologne cathedral; they regarded it as a living testament to the skill of their airmen.

On one occasion my secretary and I hitchhiked far east to Wurzburg, not far from Nuremberg and the Czechoslovakian border. The presence of a rare American female helped us flag down army trucks. Wurzburg had been flattened by aerial bombing. There at OSS's request I visited Frau Otto Kiep, a lady with the dignified, gentle manner of the German upper class and a friend of General Donovan's. Her husband had been tortured and killed in a notorious Gestapo prison in Berlin after being implicated in the 1944 putsch against Hitler. I suspected that Otto Kiep was a Crown Jewel, which would account for General Donovan's friendship. Frau Kiep was proud and had declined American offers of assistance. Later, she moved to Berlin and eventually became West Germany's consul general in Chicago under Chancellor Konrad Adenauer.

At Mannheim, up the Rhine toward Switzerland, I visited the spot where Gen. George Patton had been killed when a command vehicle blindsided him, and not far away, at Worms, I stared at the spot where Martin Luther had been hauled before the diet of the Holy Roman Empire in 1521 for his attack on various Catholic practices, including the sale of indulgences. Luther refused to recant his position and was branded a heretic, which sparked the Reformation.

In the countryside near Marburg, north of Wiesbaden, I saw the savage scars left by the U.S. Army after it had swept through like a tornado, advancing at a pace of fifty miles a day. German tanks and motor vehicles littered the sides of the roads, victims of heavy strafing and artillery fire. Most Germans were preoccupied with scavenging for wood and scarce building materials to repair their homes, tending their crops, or working on cleanup gangs in battered cities. Hitler's rusting tanks and army vehicles could wait.

In late June curiosity drew me to Frankfurt to see Eisenhower's much talked about headquarters in the I. G. Farbenindustrie's administrative building, an enormous edifice that stood mysteriously unscathed amid the rubble of the adjoining factory. Rumor had it that American bombers had spared the thing for Ike. To eyes accustomed to OSS's damaged structures in London and Wiesbaden, the facility looked unbelievably luxurious—private elevators for general officers only, pools, escalators, and modern elevators.

But most of Frankfurt lay in ruins. Block after block, the burned-out shells of buildings stood above piles of rubble eight feet high. Here and there the army had patched up a half-ruined building, but in the city center the average structure had been sheered from top to bottom by direct hits. Two or three walls might still be standing, with twisted girders and charred beams jutting from a floor and a bed or shattered bathtub dangling from a girder.

In August I spent ten days at X-2's Munich field station, seizing the opportunity to travel around Bavaria and Austria. I saw Berchtesgarden where Hitler's retreat had been smashed by bombs, and Garmisch-Partenkirchen, the scene of Hitler's 1936 winter Olympics. Garmisch was full of well-dressed, blond youngsters, the children of high German officials who had been sent there for safety. Their chubby good health sickened me when I thought of all the crimes their parents had visited on the people of Europe.

Patton's Third Army had liberated and occupied Austria, but later the United States agreed to permit the French Army to occupy part of Austria. Soon the French forbade her British and American allies to enter their zone. We heard rumors that French troops were looting the towns and treating their German prisoners harshly and didn't want any prying eyes around. An OSS captain with whom I was working in Munich suggested we drive into the French zone to see for ourselves. Apprehensive, I took some comfort in the fact that at that point we still carried Eisenhower passes assuring entry into any military installation under Eisenhower's command, which until recently meant most of northern Europe.

While we were watching a French military parade march through an Austrian town, a French lieutenant, gesticulating frantically, shouted to his commanding officer, "Americans are right over there, watching!" He accosted us, and we produced our passes. After examining them at some length, he responded with Gallic hauteur, "Well, you are in violation here, but I see this pass from General EE-sen-how-air. We will detain you no longer, but proceed directly out of the French zone, *vite vite!*"

In July I had encountered the French under very different circumstances, having been sent to Paris to talk with French intelligence about a former *Abwehr* officer whom OSS sought to recruit as an American agent in Germany. He claimed to have helped the French Resistance during the war. The French helpfully confirmed my suspicion that he was lying. I rushed through my work in order to tour Paris. The air trip over was exciting. The pilot, on noticing the air corps patch on my coat, obliged me with slight detours over the grisly battlefields of World War I. Around Metz, at low altitude, I could clearly see trenches, shell holes, and deserted forts from 1918. There were unexploded mines in the fields, and to this day large stretches of that land have not been tilled.

I was quartered in a sumptuous chateau at nearby Saint-Germain outside Paris, which lived up to its reputation as the world's most beautiful city. A Paris-based colleague of mine and I drove his Opel into the city each night for a quick look at the conventional tourist points. The city was effervescent. The cafes along the Champs Elysées overflowed with bubbly people sipping liquor, and women rode bicycles as if they could care less about the luxury of cars. In Paris, it seemed, people lived to play—all else was immaterial. But there were drawbacks. Food was still exorbitantly expensive and scarce. Buses had just started to operate. At times the French exhibited a deep inferiority complex, having recently emerged from a dark period in which each individual either suffered or compromised himself with the German occupier.

We toured Montmartre the night before Bastille Day and got swept up in the carnival spirit, passing small Ferris wheels, demonstration boxers, merry-go-rounds, and hawkers of all kinds appealing to the multitude of parading French men and women. Everywhere there was music, laughing, and excited honking as French officers tried to force their cars through the crowd.

The atmosphere was electric when returning French slave laborers and prisoners marched to L'Étoile to hear De Gaulle deliver a fervent forty-minute speech on France's emergence from bondage. Oddly, not one phrase directly or indirectly referred to Britain or the United States having been involved in the war.

The Bastille Day parade down the Champs Elysées was anticlimactic, just a smattering of people lining the boulevard, haphazardly cheering as their countrymen drove American trucks, tanks, and jeeps along the route. The French may have been tired of parades after all the fanfare on V-E Day in May, General Eisenhower's subsequent visit, and the festivities of the night before.

My OSS companion and I went to the Lido, the grandiose nightclub on the Champs Elysées where the demimonde was out in force. Prices were sky high—champagne cost fourteen dollars a bottle, a beer three—and we weren't drinking much. Bored with the show, we fell to asking one of the girls, who spoke German, about the occupation. To her, American, British, and German men were pretty much alike. If anything, the Americans were noisier and brusquer than the Germans. She said she'd been in New York once and found Americans there to be very different from Americans in Paris, who came with a preconception of the city and lived according to it during their stay.

"Didn't you hate the Germans for what they did to France?" I asked.

"Oh no."

"Why not?"

"I'm not interested in politics; many French people grew fat when the

Germans were here and now cry. The darned Boche (disparaging slang for Germans)—Why not be frank?"

Paris with its blazing lights and joie de vivre contrasted with London, which in June had banned streetlights to save fuel for the coming winter. I had a hunch that Germany would be back on its feet before France—partly because the French had been so swiftly defeated by the Germans and didn't appear to be exhibiting any self-discipline in reviving their battered economy.

But it was Berlin—not Wiesbaden or even Paris—that sparked my curiosity: Berlin, the city that had dominated world news during Hitler's twelve years in power!

South and west of Tempelhof Airport, from which German fighters had recently scrambled in the defense of the city,[1] most apartments and stores appeared unscathed by the war. Here and there roofs had collapsed under incendiaries and five-hundred-pound bombs, but on the whole the area near the airport was much more intact that any area in Frankfurt or Cologne. The heaviest destruction lay north of Tempelhof and out of sight. The most visible sign of war was a succession of twisted bridges that the *Wehrmacht* had seen fit to destroy in the last days. Street after street was blocked by lack of canal and railroad crossings.

When we had first arrived back in September, my OSS colleagues and I cleared security and drove by truck to Allied Group Control Headquarters several miles to the west in Dahlem, the smart, largely unbombed residential section where we would work. Passing through Schöneberg on the way to Dahlem, we were surprised at the light damage—worse than London's by a fair measure, but nothing crippling. The sickeningly sweet smell of death hung over the sunny streets where pedestrians, ignoring it and nearly everything else, trudged stoically about their business. They were hunting for shops where food could be found. Long queues—three and four abreast—backed up outside newly repainted grocery shops.

The next morning after interminable delays getting passes and temporary billeting, we were taken to the OSS office. Our leaders had selected a building discreetly located in a fenced-in, heavily wooded section of Dahlem at Foehrenweg 19. It was an imposing, gracefully proportioned, glazed-brick building, whose steep slate roofs displayed a large red and white cross, signifying that it had become a convalescent center late in the war. Originally, it had served as the personal headquarters of Field Marshall Wilhelm Keitel, chief of the *Wehrmacht* high command, or *Oberkommando der Wehrmacht*. The building's interior was in superb condition, befitting its former five-star occupant who, having kowtowed and assisted Hitler, was now waiting to be tried at Nuremberg as a war criminal. Keitel was ultimately convicted and hanged.

About thirty OSS staff occupied the building, including Allen Dulles, chief of mission; Richard Helms, head of SI; and my superior, Lawrence de Neufville, chief of X-2. Larry had served brilliantly in France, where, as earlier reported, his doubled *Abwehr* stay-behind agents helped deceive the Germans about the whereabouts of Patton's relief army during the Battle of the Bulge. After the fighting he conducted extensive interrogations of former top German intelligence officers. Serving with Helms in SI was Peter Sichel, an affable, bright member of a famous Rhineland wine merchant's family who, being Jewish, had fled to the United States before the war. Sichel had been brought to Berlin to relieve two discharged officers who had corrupted their espionage networks by converting them to black market operations.

Our offices spread over three floors, below which was a handy garage or "motor pool" replete with gas tanks, mechanics, and vehicles—a rarity in shattered Berlin. The living and dining accommodations were also more than adequate. Dulles, ever the genial pipe-smoking country squire, chose for his residence an elegant ivy-covered brick home at 63 A Im Dol, which, he said, was good for entertaining. As the most recent and low-ranking arrival, I drew a damaged white stucco home. The dining room ceiling hung by some means unknown to us or its plaintive owner. The windows of the bedroom were blown out, and the bathroom had large cracks, which foretold a chilly winter. Luckily the electricity worked.

We ate meals nearby in a house that had been converted into a small officer's club. We could eat in any of three rooms, on a glassed-in sun porch, or outdoors next to the lawn, listening to the strains of a small orchestra that played restful waltzes and jazz at lunch and dinner. An upstairs bar relieved Berlin's alcohol drought. We entered the dining room through the owner's library. We walked across thick carpet, stood in front of an elderly woman who looked like a kindly patron of the Junior League, paid our three or four marks (about forty cents), then sauntered into dinner, where a pretty girl in her twenties escorted us to our table. All these German women spoke impeccable English, even the hat-check girls, who looked as if they had walked in off Fifth Avenue.

I frequently drove around the sprawling, heavily populated city.[2] Its 341 square miles exceeded the area of Los Angeles. Berlin had been the strategic center of German military, industrial, and political power and, as such, had come to dominate Europe.[3] Scenes of Hitler's rise and fall lay all around, including the burned-out *Reichstag* where a fire, set by Nazis, but attributed to the Communists, helped Hitler seize power in 1933, and the ruined chancellory, or *Reichskanzlei*, where he committed suicide.

In some areas of the city, buildings stretched block after block like a long monotonous ochre-colored box, unimaginatively severe. Berlin's true beauty—that is, before the war erased it—lay in broad avenues like Unter den Linden and Potsdammerstrasse; Wilheminian palaces; museums, opera houses, and symphony halls; and the many lakes surrounded by large parks dotted with birches and scotch pines. Some called Berlin the Venice of the North, or the City of Lakes.

During the latter part of the six-year war, both the western Allies and the Soviets had ferociously punished Berlin. American and British bombing killed 52,000 Berliners, more than eight times as many people as had died in London during German bombing raids. Soviet armies killed another 100,000 with tank and artillery fire as they surged toward Hitler's bunker in the one-hundred-day Battle for Berlin in 1945.[4] By war's end Berlin's population had shrunk by a third to three million.

It was this bombed-out city that the British, Americans, and Soviets had agreed in London in 1944 should be occupied by their troops, plus those of the French. When I arrived in September 1945, the city's twenty districts had been divvied up as follows: eight to the Soviets; six to the Americans; four to the British, and two to the French.[5]

I drove around Berlin every Sunday, often taking along SSU visitors from Wiesbaden or Washington for "Cutler ruin and destruction tours."[6] With a jeep or car, I could go wherever the rubble had been swept back from the streets by thousands of *Truemmerfrauen,* or rubble-women. They would form a long line and pass bricks down the line to the last person, who placed them on a growing stack extending across the sidewalk.

In the *Stadt Mitte,* or city center, where the final battle had raged most fiercely, I found abandoned tanks, their surfaces carved like butter by the hot shells that finally stopped them. Looking down on the center from the top of the two-hundred-foot Victory column near the Tiergarten, I could see block upon block of roofless buildings, their walls crumbling slowly away. The spectacle on a short trip from the Tiergarten to Hitler's chancellory shocked me. All trees in the Tiergarten had been cut down; gangs of men were sawing the stumps for firewood. The only undamaged building to my right was an eight-story, extraordinarily thick, concrete antiaircraft or flak tower from which the last German shots were fired. On my left was the burned-out *Reichstag,* and ahead stood the dominating Brandenburg Gate, through which Hitler's troops had marched as they goose-stepped down Unter den Linden. The American embassy was a shell. Alongside it, the Adlon Hotel boasted one surviving room. German tanks littered the center of the avenue (the Russians had removed theirs—lest they be seen.)

A favorite spot to gawk at was Hitler's infamous chancellory. Soldiers from all the occupying armies flocked there on Sundays. The rooms inside were dank, dark, and in a state of disrepair. We sought out the garden where Hitler had ordered his guards to burn and bury his body after he shot himself and the living quarters underground where the propaganda minister, Joseph Goebbels, his wife, and four children drank cyanide. The Russians had looted anything movable, but ignored Hitler's personal Nazi Party stationery. I took away many samples, later writing a Christmas letter on it to my mother, which I stamped with his postage-free Hitler stamp before adding a U.S. stamp.

Not far from Hitler's chancellory lay the remains of the once-massive *Anhalter Bahnhof,* or train station, from which trains ran to the east and south. Sometimes I stopped there to photograph the wounded German soldiers being released by their Russian captors. Many had lost a leg and were using crude crutches to hobble about. All looked emaciated, their faces shrunken, their skin yellow. Blackened eye sockets undoubtedly came from lack of sleep during long journeys on cattle trains from Soviet prison camps. I might have been a Union trooper in Atlanta in 1865, gazing at Confederate soldiers, dirty, broken, and wounded, and I wouldn't have taken the photographs had they not struck me as historically important. One Russian officer appeared several times in the background of my rangefinder. I asked him whether he would like to have his picture taken. "Oh, no, never," he said, adding with a chuckle that I should "take more pictures of the master race."[7]

We Americans were drawn like magnets toward the Russian troops, especially in the Soviet sector of the city. In the early months we liked the Russians the most of the occupying forces. Their country had exercised unexpected and decisive military power, and in their willingness to try anything, they more closely resembled Americans than the gentlemanly French and British. No French or British officer would ever help repair a vehicle. That was for enlisted men. Russians were different. Russian officers would often pitch in and act like other ranks. They laughed a lot, were jolly, and responded to Americans with great curiosity. I guess we each sensed that we were the two most powerful countries in the world, and that the sun had set on the British, however courageous they might be. As for the French, their reputation was colored by the fact that they had collapsed and been rescued by the Americans and British in the west and Russians in the east.

But there was another side to the Russians, and the Germans never let us forget it. During our first months in Berlin, the Germans talked incessantly about Russian looting and raping. After conquering the city, the Soviet Army gave their troops three days to take revenge. Then discipline was restored. During those three hellish days, Berliners said, the Russians had two favorite occupations. They raped women of any age and captured or looted as many watches as possible. Russians would demand a watch, or "Uri," their corruption of the German word for watch, *Uhr*. Again and again, Berliners spoke of Soviet soldiers demanding watches when they already wore several on each wrist. Refusal inevitably invited a blow to the head.

Despite the repeated stories of Soviet depredations, we Americans took them with a grain of salt. We were fresh from viewing pictures of the Germans' horrible treatment of defenseless Jews in Auschwitz, Dachau, and other concentration camps. Moreover, there seemed to be an ulterior purpose in the German whining: arousing the Americans into opposition against the Russians. Many Berliners naively believed that the United States might be willing to fight the Russians or push them out of Berlin, when in fact the United States was rapidly demobilizing most of the four million servicemen it had sent to Europe.

We had difficulty locating Jewish citizens, the only Berliners for whom we felt great sympathy. Before the war 170,000 Jews had resided in Berlin. Now only five thousand remained. They were ill fed, bedraggled, and worse off than other Germans because they had been hounded out of their jobs long before the collapse. Many were homeless, having spent years moving from place to place to avoid detection by the Gestapo.

The Jews I did meet were mostly German-Jewish émigrés who had become SSU personnel. From them I learned the history of Jews in Germany. In ancient days the Romans, to rid themselves of an irritating thorn in their side, had transported Jews from Palestine to Germany. These Diaspora Jews settled in towns along the Rhine—they came to Cologne about 300 AD—and became merchants. In the Middle Ages, to escape periodic German persecutions, many Jews moved to Poland at the invitation of a liberal Polish king who valued their ability to read and write. Appalled by the illiteracy and backwardness in Poland, the Polish Jews stuck together and continued to speak German, which in time became known as Yiddish. Yiddish was spoken throughout Poland and Russia, but never in Spain, since Jews there had emigrated from the Middle East, not Germany.

Outside of Berlin I saw additional raw evidence of the war. *Luftwaffe* head Herman Göring had built a large villa, Carinhall, north of Berlin, where he stored part of his large collection of looted European art. Carinhall lay some fifty miles inside Soviet territory, on the road to Stettin, and western Allies were not welcome.

I joined several intrepid comrades on a jaunt to visit Göring's lair. We calculated the risk. Some Russians, we believed, would still regard us as friendly allies rather than adversaries. To lessen the chance that we would be blocked, we planned to travel in a huge American command car whose size, we hoped, would suggest great status and fend off lower-ranking Soviet soldiers from challenging our passage. So off we went.

Our trip was a journey back through time. Not far from Berlin we encountered a long line of massive Soviet tanks proceeding single file next to the road, followed by nineteenth-century wagons piled high with hay—fodder for the horses the Soviets still used for some transportation. Forty of the mammoth tanks were in one convoy, which we passed at a snail's pace, held up by a Russian hay cart convoy going in the opposite direction. The Russians' freshly painted green tanks carried up to ten soldiers on their sloping side, plus beds, bicycles, bureaus, and clothes, usually wrapped in bundles. Hardly any soldiers noticed us, but when they did, they stared in amazement at our imposing command car and three women in uniform.

When we reached Carinhall we discovered that the SS had dynamited the structure two hours before the arrival of Soviet troops in April. Despite our status as intruders, we were able to poke around the ruins, savoring the magnificent *allee* of trees and imagining the former opulence of this Valhalla built by the Nazis' greatest looter.

For the trip back, we had planned not to stop at any highway barrier where Soviet sentries might challenge us. Instead, we would drive full speed ahead, relying on the intimidating appearance of our oversized car to prevent the customary tree trunk—a makeshift Russian barrier across the road—from blocking our passage. Coming from Berlin, this stratagem had worked; at each checkpoint Soviet soldiers raised the barrier at the last moment, and we whisked through. But this time we had a close shave. Shortly before approaching one checkpoint, we came on the same tank column we had encountered before, except that now it was accompanied by a Russian general. We raced past the column, only to see him turn his head and then abruptly start off in hot pursuit. But his vehicle wasn't as fast as ours. We flew toward the gate, it snapped up, and we whizzed through, heading back to the safety of Berlin. Except along the autobahn to the west, to which Americans had access by treaty rights, I never ventured into the Soviet zone again.

Maj. Gen. "Wild Bill" Donovan was chief of the Office of Strategic Services (OSS) and close to President Franklin Roosevelt. *National Archives*

A present day photograph of the old London headquarters of the OSS's counterintelligence branch, X-2, at 14 Ryder Street near Picadilly Circus. X-2 shared the building with part of Section V of MI-6. *Martyn Gregory*

Norman Holmes Pearson, a Yale English instructor on leave, was X-2 chief for Europe. *Yale University Collection of American Literature, Beinecke Library*

After Germany's surrender, the OSS established a headquarters in the German resort city of Wiesbaden, where the author was transferred in June 1945. The OSS office was housed in the Henkel Truecken *sekt* (sparkling wine) plant pictured here. *Author's Collection*

Pictured here in Wiesbaden are, from left to right, Hugh Cunningham; Wilma Taber, the author's assistant in London; and the author. *Author's Collection*

Berlin's war-damaged Brandenburg Gate in November 1945. This gate was on the frontline between western Berlin and the Soviet sector. *Author's Collection*

Berlin's imposing anti-aircraft tower in the Tiergarten, where the last shots of the war in Europe were fired. *Author's Collection*

Berlin women stacking rubble in the Soviet sector, a common sight after the war. *Author's Collection*

Karl Johann Wiberg, a Swede who had maintained a business in Berlin throughout the war, was an OSS sub-agent. Wiberg used his store to cache weapons and his apartment as a potential safe haven for OSS agents. *Cornelius Ryan Collection, Ohio University*

Richard Helms, pictured here years later, was chief of the Strategic Services Unit's (SSU) Berlin Station in November and December 1945. *Central Intelligence Agency*

Heinz Krull served in the Abwehr's counterespionage branch during the war. After the war, working under the codename "Zig-Zag," he helped U.S. counterintelligence turn many Germans who were spying for the Soviets into American double agents. *Heinz Krull*

Hans Kemritz, an Abwehr major during the war, lured former German intelligence officers out of hiding so the Soviet NKVD could capture them. Krull convinced Kemritz to become a double agent for the Americans. Kemritz provided the Americans with invaluable information about the activities of Soviet intelligence in Berlin until he was forced to go into hiding. *Illustrierte Berliner Zeitung*

Joe House, a villa at 5 Promenadenstrasse in Berlin's Steglitz district, was where American agents stayed while reporting back on assignments in the Soviet Zone. *Author's Collection*

The author's Tatra car that he used to transport a Soviet intelligence defector out of Berlin. *Author's Collection*

SSU agents dining at Joe House. *Author's Collection*

The Soviet officers who invited the author to a drinking party. *Author's Collection*

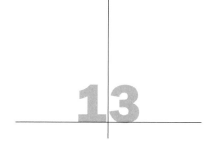

COUNTERESPIONAGE
CASE OFFICER

Now that Truman had terminated OSS and our former enemy was vanquished, what was the mission of X-2? At first, we carried on with the logical extension of wartime duties, tracking German intelligence personnel, interrogating them to find out what they might have done to captured American spies, and figuring out how our old adversaries, the *Abwehr* and *Sicherheitsdienst*, had operated. Some of the worst offenders might warrant prosecution. Others might be held as witnesses in war crimes trials scheduled to begin in November.

In addition, SI sought to learn what the Soviets were doing in their occupied zone that they didn't tell their Allies about, such as transporting German jets and jet factories back to the Soviet Union.[1]

About one half of X-2 personnel in Germany had been sent home by October.[2] Berlin's remaining X-2 staff included Laurence de Neufville, Sgt. Floyd Johnson, Hugh Montgomery, and myself. De Neufville "ran," or acted as spymaster for, some X-2 agents, while Johnson and Montgomery helped with lesser ones. Soon, Johnson left and de Neufville went on leave, returning to Berlin a month later to become director of intelligence at the Office of Military Government. When Montgomery went back to Harvard in late November, he was replaced by Tom Polgar, a talented young linguist. Polgar had left Hungary in 1938 to study in the United States. After Pearl Harbor he joined the U.S. Army as an enemy alien upon the personal intervention of Eleanor Roosevelt and became an instant American citizen.

Because I was a first lieutenant and Polgar a sergeant, I was suddenly—to my amazement—in charge of X-2. My total inexperience in the direct management of agents reflected the level to which SSU counteres-pionage capacity had shrunk. The only way to go was up, by learning fast and adding personnel below me. According to revised army estimates, I would be eligible to go home sometime in 1946. Meanwhile, I would rel-ish the long-deferred excitement of working directly with agents.

I inherited a handful of minor agents, and that was just as well. They provided me with an opportunity to learn so that I wouldn't compromise American security when I made the inevitable beginner's mistakes. One was Barbara Güttler, a vivacious former secretary at the Paris office of the *Abwehr* who spoke and wrote fluent English and French. The Americans had imprisoned her father as a possible war criminal. Her first SSU han-dler had the blunt and foolish notion that she would be more apt to work for the Americans because we could threaten, if we chose, to make it hard for her captive father. Coercion repelled me. Besides, the Russians' heavy reliance on it in recruiting agents often worked against them. Barbara was anxious to help anyway. The challenge was to find a suitable intelligence assignment for her. Unfortunately, I never did.

Nonetheless, the companionship of Barbara and her aristocratic Sile-sian mother, with whom she shared a small apartment, was welcome. They contributed mightily to my growing German vocabulary, confi-dence in speaking the language, and knowledge of what Germans thought about Hitler and his aggressive war. They would joke about my child-like sentences and words and dubbed me "Puttiput,"—the name, they said, of an appealing young chicken who was always getting into trouble in a well-known German fable.

One night Barbara went downstairs to say goodbye to me on the gar-den walk just outside her door. It was a few minutes after the 9 PM curfew, and immediately American military police swooped down on us and arrested her. My hands were tied. I couldn't prevent her being jailed with-out disclosing my relationship as her (potential) spymaster and destroy-ing any usefulness she might have. So, I shamefacedly let the MPs carry her off without a protest, then dashed upstairs to inform her mother what had happened. Barbara spent the night on the concrete floor of jail in the company of two prostitutes and a recently released, homeless German prisoner of war. At least the jail was heated, and my recruit was released the next day. Mother and daughter laughed about the incident.

Another agent did have a mission. She was a woman who owned and ran a school to teach German secretaries sufficient English to gain sought-after employment with the American military government. Her role was to spot any students who might be Soviet spies. Already, we were concerned that the Soviet intelligence service, NKVD, was seeking to unlock American secrets by suborning German secretaries for top army officers. My spymaster predecessor had promised her preferential coal supplies in a city where that primary source of heat had all but ceased to exist. I'm not sure I knew the extent of his unwritten promise to her, but later she became angry that I had not fulfilled her expectations.

She complained not to me but, without my knowledge, to the CIC, possibly believing that the CIC's power was superior to our own. She dropped out of sight for three days, leading us to fear that the Russians had captured her. Instead, the CIC had detained her for questioning about our spy operation at her school and learned the names of two of our minor agents. CIC's unseemly curiosity may have been stimulated by competitive jealousy about our far greater role in clandestine intelligence. Sensing she was disloyal and knew more than an ingrate should, we decided to ship her out of Berlin. Fortunately, an SSU staff officer from Washington was touring Germany. I arranged for her to escort the offending spy to Munich, then had the school closed down.

A third agent was more significant. He was Karl Johann Wiberg, a subagent of the Dane Jessen-Schmidt, who, the reader might recall, had operated as an OSS agent inside Germany toward the end of the war. Wiberg, a Swedish businessman who had maintained a business in Berlin throughout the war, was fortyish, pale, smoked constantly, and drank heavily. My superiors understated his wartime assignment to me. They said only that during the war he had made his apartment a safe haven for any OSS spy who might parachute into Berlin. Sometimes spies were injured on landing and needed medical attention, as well as a place in which to hide from Gestapo pursuers. I had no need to know his precise wartime role, and Wiberg was reticent about it. I assumed it had been rather bland.

Years later, to my surprise, I found out differently, and in a strange roundabout manner. In the 1960s Wiberg had the misfortune of being interviewed by Cornelius Ryan, author of *The Last Battle*, which described the Soviet Army's bloody final assault on Berlin. According to Ingeborg Mueller, Wiberg's live-in secretary and later his wife, Ryan promised he would not use her husband's name in his book, but broke his promise. At any rate, Ryan described Wiberg's role as far more significant than I had ever imagined:[3]

This Swede who was more German than the Germans was also a member of America's top-secret Office of Strategic Services. He was an Allied spy. . . .

Wiberg had been notified by his superior, a Dane named Hennings Jessen-Schmidt, that henceforth he was to be a "storekeeper" for the spy network in Berlin. [Thereafter,] he had received a variety of supplies through couriers. . . . His phone would ring twice, then stop; that was the signal that a delivery was to be made. The supplies arrived only after the hours of darkness, and generally during an air raid. . . . His apartment was now a virtual warehouse of espionage equipment. Cached in his rooms were a large quantity of currency, some code tables, and a variety of drugs and poisons—from quick-acting "knock out" pellets . . . to deadly cyanide compounds. In his coal cellar and a rented garage nearby was a small arsenal of rifles, revolvers, and ammunition. Wiberg even had a suitcase of highly volatile explosives. . . . He and Jensen-Schmidt had found the perfect hiding place. The explosives were now in a large safety box at the Deutsche Union Bank.

Wiberg's apartment had miraculously survived the air raids up to now, but he dreaded to think of the consequences if he were hit. He would be immediately exposed. Jessen-Schmidt had told Wiberg that at the right time, the supplies would be issued to various groups of operatives and saboteurs who would shortly arrive in Berlin. The operations of these selected agents were to begin on the receipt of a signal sent either by radio or through the courier network from London. Wiberg expected the distribution to be made soon. Jessen-Schmidt had been warned to stand by for the message some time during the next few weeks, for the work of the teams would coincide with the capture of the city. According to the information Jessen-Schmidt and Wiberg had received, the British and Americans would reach Berlin about the middle of April.

According to what he had heard at the food shop, Hitler was definitely in the Berlin area—at a headquarters in Bernau, only about fourteen miles northeast of the city. . . . By the afternoon of Wednesday, April 18, a message was en route to London. . . . Wiberg fervently hoped the Allies would act on his report. . . . What better present could they give him [Hitler] for his fifty-sixth birthday, April 20, than a massive air raid.[4]

After publication of Ryan's book, Wiberg was ostracized by his German friends and customers and suffered a severe financial reversal. Over the years, his wife recalled less and less of his intelligence past. We corresponded frequently. She ultimately wrote me that his only role had been as consul for the Swedes after the war.[5] Her denial, I believe, was born of the pain that she and Wiberg suffered because Ryan published that he was an American spy during the bombing of Berlin.

In any event, I obtained coal rations for Wiberg and provided supplementary food from the U.S. Post Exchange. For eleven months he fed me continuous intelligence about conditions inside the Soviet Union. He had become the Swedish consul and was in close touch with compatriots who had been captured in Berlin by Soviet troops, taken to Moscow, and subsequently released to find their way back. Coming to him for help on their return, they eagerly reported to him what they had seen passing through the Soviet Union and Poland, such as Soviet troop movements and the availability and prices of food and supplies. It was low-level intelligence at best, but at X-2 we and our superiors in Wiesbaden and Washington welcomed any scrap of information revealing what the mysterious Soviets were up to. Russia proved to be exactly what Churchill said it was: "A riddle wrapped inside a mystery inside an enigma."[6]

We did need capable spies to penetrate Soviet secrecy. While I learned much from working with minor agents like Wiberg, OSS veterans schooled me in analytical and espionage techniques. One was Richard Helms, who had become head of the Berlin base after Allen Dulles returned home in the fall. He exuded the warm friendliness of a Midwesterner and had a disarming smile. Before joining OSS, Helms had been a newspaper reporter with the United Press in Europe and had interviewed Hitler. He had a journalist's keen nose for facts, as well as an admirable management and training style. Whenever I proposed to Helms how to solve a particular espionage problem, such as deciding an agent's next move, he was courteous, crisp, imaginative, and above all, sensible.

From Helms I learned a lifelong lesson in the advantages of comparative analysis. He once said, "Dick, I can better judge whether your recommended solution is the best if you carefully describe the top two possible alternative solutions, analyze the pros and cons of each, and then tell me why you picked number one over number two. That approach gives depth to your analysis not available if you only present the case for the winner."

Especially helpful were frequent, long sessions in which the head of British MI-6 counterespionage in Berlin, Maj. L. F. Brydon, and I shared our recent operations involving Soviet intelligence. A bachelor like me, he offset the loneliness of his secret work with a pet dog, a distinct rarity in food-short Berlin. Brydon was a quiet operative who had considerable experience with counterespionage. In the fall of 1945 he was already working with the first defectors from the Soviet intelligence system. I admired British skill in attracting those defectors and hoped I could do the same. MI-6 also explained that they had obtained extensive intelligence from Russian slave laborers held in Germany.

Some may be born with a knack for counterespionage, but certain skills can be developed only in actual operations. For me, on a fast learning curve, it was sink or swim. Fortunately, close teamwork with a smart former *Abwehr* officer helped me swim.

The agent was Heinz Krull, code-named Zig-Zag, who before the war had served as a government prosecutor in his native Berlin. In 1941, on being called to military service in the *Abwehr*'s counterespionage branch, he investigated people suspected of spying. In February 1944, when Hitler dissolved the *Abwehr*, Zig-Zag's entire branch was taken over by the counterespionage section of the *Sicherheitsdienst*.[7] As Berlin crumbled before the advancing Soviet Army, Zig-Zag fled west disguised as a simple private. (When Heinrich Himmler did the same, attempting to cross over to British lines in Hamburg, he was captured and committed suicide.) Taken prisoner by the Americans, Zig-Zag promptly raised American suspicions. He wore an ill-fitting uniform and had a low military rank for someone in his mid to late thirties. CIC interrogators discovered his true identity and obtained the names of fifty-three former *Abwehr* colleagues. Then G-2 transferred him to OSS-Wiesbaden, from which he was sent to me in Berlin for use as a double agent, or agent provocateur.

Immediately, we asked Zig-Zag to track down all the former *Abwehr* officers he had known in Berlin. Many had departed forever, but some had stayed, while others had left and then returned. Zig-Zag set about his task with surprising zest. In almost no time, he discovered two or three targets. Equipped with a false name and documents, Zig-Zag told his quarries that he had fooled the "dumb Americans," or "Amis," as we were called, by posing under an alias. Then, he inquired how they had escaped capture. Being a small, inconspicuous man, Zig-Zag easily convinced most targets that he had indeed fooled the dumb Americans. All of his targets were on the occupying powers' automatic arrest list because of their former intelligence positions. Some, he found, had become agents for the NKVD.

Sometimes the NKVD took a family member hostage in order to coerce its prey to become an agent against the West, particularly against the Americans. The Soviet practice of redirecting former German intelligence personnel against the West, in addition to fractious and uncooperative Soviet occupation policies, quickly convinced OSS that the Soviet Union under Joseph Stalin was intensely hostile. As the counterespionage branch, we decided to try to identify all Soviet agents, learn their missions, neutralize them, and if possible double a select few. Zig-Zag with his superior intelligence, knowledge of Berlin, and zeal to do in the Soviets was a great find. Over several months he traced and compromised many Soviet agents from the *Abwehr*. We then doubled them ourselves or imprisoned them as members of the former German intelligence.

As Zig-Zag continued ferreting out Soviet agents, I learned step by step how to play cat and mouse with their intelligence system. He taught me deception methods such as the use of cutouts, or go-betweens, who add security to an operation by passing information between the spy and the person controlling his or her assignment. This helps prevent an enemy agent who is tailing a spy from discovering his controller.

Zig-Zag also improved my German. Being a typical Prussian, he respected authority and took all commands literally. I would say, "Correct my German whenever I use a wrong word or sentence structure— even right in the middle of our conversation."

"*Ja wohl, Herr Oberleutnant,* I shall do so."

Never were truer words spoken. After I became a captain in March, Zig-Zag was constantly interrupting my German conversation with, "*Herr Hauptmann, Sie haben einen anderen Fehler gemacht. Das richtiges Wort ist . . .*" meaning, "Mr. Captain, you have made another mistake. The right word is . . ."

To protect Zig-Zag we were constantly changing his aliases and false documents and did so fifteen times in all. We tried to search for ex-*Abwehr* officers not in current contact with former colleagues recently apprehended by us; otherwise, they might be suspicious of Zig-Zag. It was a dangerous game. If identified by the NKVD, Zig-Zag would be quickly kidnapped and killed or imprisoned under the pretext that he was a wanted SS officer. In fact, the time did come when the number of former *Abwehr* officers turned Soviet agents dwindled to such an extent that Zig-Zag's detection became inevitable. But that lay in the future.

Weekly reports to Washington noted by early October that we had four double agents, sometimes called penetration agents, who were all former *Abwehr* officers recruited by the NKVD and then doubled by us. One, code-named "Moccasin," was an NKVD agent who "had produced information on the organization of the NKVD Berlin, its units, and personnel through most useful friendships with General Mikelewitsch and Col. Antonivic."[8]

The Soviets apparently suspected that Moccasin was also working for us and attempted to assassinate him. I cabled SSU-Wiesbaden using our one-time top-secret code. The message, countersigned by Richard Helms, read,

1. Moccasin memory temporarily gone.
2. Being visited hospital Russian officers.
3. Leaves hospital next week when will see.
4. Two other CIC informants, each Communists, same neighborhood attacked since Moccasin was. CIC investigating but unable curb reprisals as yet.[9]

Today, I have no recollection of the unfortunate Moccasin's ultimate fate, but he was probably imprisoned or killed. He worked for us just briefly. I would never have seen him as his reports came to us through Zig-Zag.

Another of our agents was code-named "Savoy." If the Moccasin operation was short-lived, Savoy's lasted for more than two years, producing useful intelligence, but at a great price to be paid years later. Savoy was a former *Abwehr* major, Hans Kemritz, whom Zig-Zag easily located and doubled almost as soon as Kemritz returned to his prewar law office in the Soviet sector of Berlin, near the Brandenburg Gate. When Zig-Zag hinted to Kemritz that there were advantages to becoming an American agent, his quarry replied, "But I'm already working for the NKVD." Zig-Zag countered, "You could work for the Americans by telling them what the Soviets are asking you to do." He did.

Kemritz had a rich past. He had served as a combat officer in World War I, joined the Nazi party in 1933, and become a successful lawyer in private practice. In 1939 the German Army recalled Kemritz to duty and assigned him to the *Abwehr* counterespionage directorate in Berlin, where he ultimately became chief of III-F, responsible for the security of military personnel. Kemritz was captured by the Soviet Army on May 1, 1945, and imprisoned in Berlin. He was interrogated relentlessly, allowed only four hours of sleep nightly, and lost considerable weight. One NKVD captain, who said his name was Skurin and whose real name we never learned, released Kemritz in October 1945 on condition that he become an agent for the NKVD and not leave the Soviet sector of Berlin.

The NKVD ordered Kemritz to locate men they were looking for, primarily former *Abwehr* officers. Kemritz immediately wrote letters from his old law office to *Abwehr* colleagues and other Berlin lawyers. He invited them to come to his office, sometimes for a social chat, sometimes on pretended legal business. Kemritz reported to Skurin the time when they were to arrive. After leaving Kemritz's office they were arrested by Skurin and hauled off to the same jail in which Kemritz had been confined. They were interrogated and often accused, in these instances falsely, of being American spies.

We considered Kemritz to be a potentially valuable double agent. A highly experienced intelligence officer with many acquaintances in Berlin, he was smart, confident, and daring to the point of recklessness. He worked diligently for Captain Skurin. The more targets he fingered for Skurin, the more he was asked to nominate and locate. He could help us learn more about this Captain Skurin, whom we came to believe was a key figure in anti-American espionage. We asked Zig-Zag to obtain from Kemritz as much information as possible about Skurin's intelligence objectives and colleagues.

Kemritz met frequently with Skurin to suggest or learn what new unwary person should be lured into the Soviet net, either outside his office or, when that became too risky, inside some government office to which the prey had been summoned. Gradually, Kemritz fed a stream of significant information to Zig-Zag about Skurin's objectives, methods, and colleagues. Kemritz even handed Zig-Zag copies of the written reports he prepared for Skurin.

Skurin's targets were subject to automatic arrest by any of the occupying powers. The Americans sometimes imprisoned captured *Abwehr* officers for a year. That was the fate accorded one von Hake whom Zig-Zag had identified to the CIC in Frankfurt. The Soviets treated captured Nazi intelligence officers more harshly. Once, with our approval, Zig-Zag warned von Hake—after he was released by the Americans and returned to Berlin—to avoid Kemritz's office because it was a trap. Von Hake ignored Zig-Zag's warning and paid the price.

By mid-1946 Kemritz had provided 90 percent of the information gathered by SSU about Soviet intelligence in Berlin, thanks to Skurin's relentless intelligence operations. Inevitably, however, the disappearance of so many Germans immediately after contact with Kemritz led to his undoing. On November 2, 1945, only three weeks after being released from the NKVD prison, he had arranged for two appointments at different times with Erich Klose, a personnel officer of the *Abwehr*, and Wolf von Gersdorff, an *Abwehr* driver in Romania. Both were hauled off to the same Soviet jail where Kemritz had been imprisoned. There Skurin struck von Gersdorff in the face, falsely accused him of being a spy for the Americans, and placed him in painfully cramped solitary confinement. Eventually, when von Gersdorff's weight dropped to one hundred pounds, he was sent to a Berlin hospital. There, in return for release, he agreed to Skurin's "proposal" that he spy on the Americans. Instead, von Gersdorff made a beeline for the Americans, who quickly settled him and his family in West Germany for their security.[10] His cellmate was not so lucky. He died in prison weeks after von Gersdorff's release.

Many of Kemritz's other victims who landed in Soviet prisons, like von Hake, died there. The wives of Kemritz's victims, including Elly von Hake, soon linked Kemritz to the disappearances. Individually, they made inquiries of the Soviet occupiers, who denied knowledge of the disappearances. By August 1946 the U.S. military government (unaware that Kemritz was an American double agent) said they would try to stop Kemritz, though they were powerless to arrest him legally in the Soviet sector where he remained. Then, the women found out about each other and started holding regular meetings, pooling their efforts to hunt him down.

In late 1947 Kemritz disappeared from Berlin after jeopardizing his position with the NKVD. He had negligently noted on one of his reports to the NKVD that a copy had been made for American intelligence. SSU promptly moved him to West Germany.

In 1950 Elly von Hake sued Kemritz in a Berlin civil court for damages for the loss of her husband.[11] She was supported by the *Kampfgruppe gegen Unmenschlichkeit*, a vigilant anti-Soviet human rights activist group that was subsequently financed by the CIA. By that time two major events had raised the Cold War to a fever pitch. One was the Soviet Army's 1947 move into Czechoslovakia. The other was Stalin's attempt to starve the Western powers out of Berlin by cutting off their land access, which the Americans and British thwarted by flying in food and fuel in the 1948 Berlin airlift.

Kemritz's eventual undoing came, not from Elly von Hake, but from one of his first victims, Wolf von Gersdorff, who discovered that his nemesis had moved from Berlin to Bad Hamburg in West Germany, brazenly resumed his law practice under his real name, and been elected mayor. Von Gersdorff persuaded the state of Hesse to prosecute Kemritz for assisting in his "illegal detention" and that of others. On November 1, 1950, Kemritz was arrested and admitted to the district judge that he had delivered von Gersdorff to the Russians, but claimed that he was only obeying orders of higher authority. He irritated the judge by stating that an unnamed authority would release him the next day.[12]

That didn't happen. The right of the emerging German government to prosecute him had already been approved by the pro-German U.S. high commissioner, John J. McCloy. Soon the head of the CIA in Germany, retired Lt. Gen. Lucian K. Trucott vigorously appealed to McCloy not to sacrifice an agent who had served the United States.[13] McCloy agreed and ordered the Kemritz case transferred to the U.S. prosecutor in Berlin. Kemritz was released on bail and given a prominent defense lawyer, Robert Kempner, the American chief prosecutor, no less, during the later rounds of the Nuremberg war crime trials.

While the American prosecutor investigated Kemritz, a Berlin magazine, *IBZ (Illustrierte Berliner Zeitung)*, stirred the pot. In the spring of 1951, in a seven-installment article entitled "The Scale of Justice," it reported that Kemritz had sent twenty Germans to Russian prisons where many died. The article created a sensation, making Kemritz's case a cause célèbre. Germans threw rocks through his villa windows and sent postcards addressed to "NKVD agent Dr. Kemritz."

On June 14, 1951, the U.S. prosecutor terminated the case against Kemritz. The U.S. high commissioner announced that Kemritz had rendered a valuable service to American security, that all the Germans he sent into Soviet hands were on the automatic arrest list promulgated by the Allies, and that the arrests were made by an agency of an occupying power. The decision validating Kemritz's acts—because done pursuant to the occupiers' laws—became known in German history as Lex Kemritz. Hans Kemritz and his wife were moved that same day to a U.S. Army camp for their protection.

The American policy infuriated Germans; it seemed to say, "hands off, we know best." Deputies in the German *Bundestag* demanded that Kemritz be tried in courts and criticized the American occupying forces as never before. A lengthy *New York Times* account caught my attention in Milwaukee, where I was living at the time. It said that the popular West Berlin Mayor, Ernst Reuter, had railed against U.S. policy and that von Hake's widow was demanding compensation for the loss of her husband. On August 14, 1951, I wrote to High Commissioner McCloy as chairman of the Milwaukee Branch of the Foreign Policy Association. After acknowledging that I had recruited Kemritz, I suggested that the United

States should protect its agents and show magnanimity by giving Frau von Hake compensation for the loss of her husband.

The CIA removed Kemritz and his wife to the United States in 1952 and later settled them in Uruguay, where the former *Abwehr* officer lived until his death. Eventually, my letter to McCloy found its way to the National Archives in Washington, where an enterprising German investigative reporter found it in 2000. She called me from Berlin, eventually interviewed me, and referred to my letter and interview in an hour-long radio broadcast, "Kidnapping: The Double Game of Lawyer Hans Kemritz," on the fiftieth anniversary of McCloy's announcement of Lex Kemritz.[14]

Undeterred by Moccasin's assassination in the fall of 1945, Zig-Zag continued to be diligent and as sharp-nosed as a hunting dog. He located former *Abwehr* officers turned Soviet agents almost as rapidly as the heavily manned Soviet intelligence system minted them. After we neutralized several Soviet agents through Zig-Zag, it was only a matter of time before the Soviets would suspect that he was more than the former unapprehended and unallied *Abwehr* officer he pretended to be. Increasingly, Zig-Zag's targets would exhibit more than customary nervousness when meeting him and engaging in the usual exchange of stories about escaping arrest by the conquering armies. We changed Zig-Zag's aliases and matching documents each time we neutralized one of the newly created Soviet agents he had spotted for us. He simply disappeared, only to pop up later with a new name, job, and residential quarters.

I vividly remember an episode involving a valuable Soviet agent. His conversations with Zig-Zag being guarded, we felt he might be suspicious of him. He was certainly more circumspect and therefore more dangerous than the average former German intelligence officer. We wanted to apprehend him and sensed that the Soviets wanted to do the same to Zig-Zag. In fact, we assumed there might be a simultaneous effort by each side to capture the other's agent on the occasion of their next rendezvous. The Soviet agent lived a half block from an American Red Cross canteen where women often served coffee to the troops on the sidewalk. We designated someone to arrest the supposed Soviet agent as he walked toward his apartment, where he had agreed to meet Zig-Zag. The person making the arrest would be alerted to the agent's approach on the sidewalk by a hand signal from Zig-Zag nearby. Suspecting that the Soviet agent, when confronted, would bolt and run away, we planned to deter him by a swift show of overwhelming force. How to arrange the trap without tipping him off?

My brainchild seems laughable now, but I was dead serious then. I reasoned that it would not appear unusual for an off-duty American tank to stop by the canteen for coffee. The Red Cross girls would drape themselves over the tank as they normally did while serving doughnuts and coffee to the crew. Zig-Zag would shout to the Soviet agent, "You're under arrest. Come with me, that tank is covering you." Arranging the short-term loan of a tank was easy. I asked the G-2 colonel who had been so cooperative with the NKVD defector Vladimir for one, which he happily provided—at an undisclosed price.

Meanwhile, I rehearsed with Zig-Zag. He was terribly nervous, chewing his stubby nails more than usual. He was the bait that could be caught, although the presence of the tank would be somewhat reassuring. We both lost sleep.

On the appointed day, Zig-Zag arrived on cue. The Soviet agent appeared when expected and started walking warily down the block. Before he got close enough for Zig-Zag to give the hand signal that he was approaching, our target noticed an American colonel in full uniform standing next to the tank; our G-2 colonel couldn't miss the show he had helped arrange. The agent reversed direction, abruptly disappeared around a corner, and never rose to Zig-Zag's bait again. That was the end of their rendezvous.

Soon thereafter, Zig-Zag had a close call. One day he arrived at a meeting with me visibly shaken and burst forth, "*Herr Oberleutnant*, they nearly captured me! Last night I met that new find I talked to you about. We had supper together at the restaurant. I learned about his present occupation, but he wouldn't tell me where he lived or worked. It seemed fishy. Then I took the S Bahn to my neighborhood and was walking toward my apartment when I heard an engine running. I stopped and listened. It was an auto engine. No one in Berlin wastes gasoline like that except Russians or Americans. So I turned back and went elsewhere for the night."

We arranged for army enlisted men to inspect Zig-Zag's apartment, feeling a kidnaper might be lying in wait. The place had been utterly ransacked—mattress ripped apart, sheets shredded, bureau drawers emptied. This put an end to Zig-Zag's ability to roll up the Soviet espionage net. The question was, how could we protect his safety and still take advantage of his skill?

That question was answered when Richard Helms gave me a new extraduty assignment as head of a Joe house—a house for itinerant agents—in a refurbished villa at 5 Promenadenstrasse in Berlin's Steglitz district. He explained that my SSU predecessor had been sacked for endangering security by sleeping with a maid there. I was to replace him as officer in charge.

Why a residence for spies? SI was running agents into the Soviet zone of Germany and beyond, all the way east to Warsaw and south to Prague. During the war, German spy-catchers had employed electronic gear to zero in on and neutralize any source of radio transmissions not authorized by them. Assuming the Soviets, no slouches at espionage, would do the same, SSU decided early on to protect its operations by avoiding radio transmissions altogether, except in cases of dire emergency. Any SI agent working in the Soviet-occupied area would return to Berlin periodically and be debriefed in person by his spymaster.

Life in Soviet-occupied Europe was not only hazardous for spies, it was also grim, with food, heat, clothing, medical care, and recreation all scarce. SI provided comfortable living accommodations in Berlin to encourage agents and reward them for their dangerous work. The Joe house offered good food and wine, maid service, clean linen, heated rooms—the works. In addition, SSU obtained symphony or opera tickets and located dentists and doctors to administer to the needs of their charges. A good cook, a handyman, several maids, and an American supply sergeant kept the villa running like a friendly residential club.

Of course, grouping spies with diverse assignments in one place created enormous security risks. Soviet troops were permitted to enter the American sector, where they could easily capture and torture an agent to confirm the existence of a Joe house, then cripple American espionage efforts by kidnapping a nest of spies in one fell swoop. Also, housing agents together for protracted periods might compromise the security of assignments and true identities.

"As an X-2 officer," Helms said, "you're trained to be doubly security conscious. This matter is urgent, and we'd like you to pack and go there tonight. The supply sergeant will take charge of provisioning the place; you're to dine at the table with the agents and supervise them in maintaining security and respect for our organization." He didn't need to add that I shouldn't sleep with the maids. Nor did I, although there was a tempting incident when a heavy cold confined me to bed for three days. A twentyish Fräulein brought me broth and, on each visit to my bedside, leaned so low while arranging the tray that her bosom brushed slowly across my prone, but not insensitive, form. Maybe she was the one who had enticed my predecessor to deviate from the straight and narrow.

At any rate, I decided to move Zig-Zag into the Joe house to determine whether any agents were loose lipped about their identity. That would protect Zig-Zag and the agents' security until we could better channel his talents.

Zig-Zag's new role developed quickly. He mixed with the other agents, telling them that he had a regular assignment against Soviet intelligence without divulging what it was or his true name (he was now on his fifteenth alias). He knew we were concerned about the rising number of Soviet spies in Berlin, trying to neutralize any key players we could uncover. Often we suspected that someone was an agent, but we lacked sufficient proof before acting. How could we learn more with our small staff, which was puny compared with the Soviet intelligence colossus?

One day he had a bright idea. It relied on the German propensity to obey orders. At that time, the *Kriminalpolizei,* or criminal investigation arm of the German police, was still operating throughout Berlin. If a burglar living in the American sector also operated in the Soviet sector, the police in their respective sectors would exchange information, often leading to an arrest. Zig-Zag's idea was to pose as a *Kriminalpolizei* officer from the Schöneberg District in the American sector. He would phone his *Kriminalpolizei* counterparts in the Soviet sector and give them the name of any German in that sector whom we suspected might be a Soviet spy. After announcing that the suspect was being investigated for some crime like burglary, Zig-Zag would request (and receive) a full dossier from the police—the suspect's employer, job, and residence address. Zig-Zag was a smooth operator. Using various police officer aliases, he succeeded in tracking numerous Soviet spies. We often laughed at the idea of Communist police investigating Soviet spies for the Americans.

Meanwhile, very guardedly, Zig-Zag worked on doubling one or two *Abwehr* officers against their Soviet masters. The game appeared to have become less dangerous. Knowing they knew who he was, he didn't try to conceal his identity. Instead, he spelled out why it would be in their interest to turn against the coercive Soviets. Long negotiations were required. He played on their fear and hatred of the Russians, pointing out that they were a menace to Germany and that only the United States could do anything about it. By assisting the Americans, the agent could possibly help lift the yoke of enforced Communism from his land. Besides, the United States would eventually offer him refuge if he fled his Soviet spymasters.

Zig-Zag did much of his espionage work during the day and at night helped me oversee the security of the Joe house. One night I drove back to the house just before the dinner hour. No sooner had I entered the door than several resident agents and members of the house staff rushed up to me, panic-stricken. They blurted out that several armed Russian soldiers had been going through the neighborhood stopping at houses. They were afraid that the identity of the Joe house had been discovered and that they would all be kidnapped. I thought it more likely that the Russians, rather than being on an official mission, were either AWOL or drunk and looking for loot. But my charges wouldn't be comforted. I told them I would reconnoiter outside and send the Russians away if they were there. Removing my Colt .45 from its holster for the first time since target practice at the Army Air Force Officer Candidate School in Miami two and a half years earlier, I went out into the black Berlin night.

I proceeded in a giant circle around the house, stumbling over rubble and trying to avoid caved-in basements. A slight wind rustled through the pine trees and there was an eerie metallic echo as a bathtub, still hanging from its piping, swung and clanged against a standing brick wall. I wandered about, discharging my revolver several times to assure the nervous agents inside that I was dutifully frightening off any lurking Soviet troops.

But as soon as I returned to the Joe house, bedlam broke out again. *"Zig-Zag wird verhaftet!"* they screamed. "He's gone, disappeared; they must have taken him!"

Back outside I went to resume my search, and when at last, after a long and fruitless interval, I returned to the house, Zig-Zag was safely inside. During my first foray into the night, he had gone out unauthorized and unnoticed.

"I was afraid the Russians might be following you," he explained to me. "I figured that if I trailed you at a discreet distance, I could determine if you were being followed and warn you."

That showed real courage. The Soviets would have made short shrift of a former *Sicherheitsdienst* counterespionage officer who was now working for American intelligence.

After August 1946, at which point I was no longer in the SSU, the pace of espionage operations quickened, and Zig-Zag refined his techniques. To reduce the risk of detection and kidnapping by the Soviets, he operated increasingly as a cutout between my successor as SSU spymaster and the already recruited double agent, Hans Kemritz. Thus, he no longer made the risky initial contact with former *Abwehr* officers turned Soviet agents.

But still there was risk, and sometime in 1947, when he and his handlers sensed that his capture was imminent, Zig-Zag left the American secret service. Having done more than enough for the Americans, he was handsomely rewarded. SSU's successor, the CIA, arranged a job for him with the U.S. military government in the German city of Kassel, where under a changed name he would be beyond the likely reach of Soviet retaliation. He blossomed as an intelligence analyst for the American consul general at Kassel, receiving numerous promotions and commendations.

Until 1952 Zig-Zag wrote me often from Kassel. He had developed an almost puppy dog–like appreciation for an old comrade. "Our friends have come looking for me," he once wrote. "I fear that with continued effort, they will succeed." Maybe the intense publicity about the Kemritz case in 1951 helped the NKVD trace Zig-Zag. He didn't need to be told what the Soviets would do if they found him. I immediately contacted my former boss Sidney Lennington, then in the CIA, told him of Zig-Zag's letter, and reminded him how Zig-Zag had repeatedly risked his life for our cause.

Within three months, the CIA had brought Zig-Zag to the United States to become an American citizen. The July 1947 statute creating the CIA authorized it to bring up to one hundred aliens into the United States each year as a reward for their contribution to national security. The law specifically exempted the CIA's aliens from laws banning entry to members of criminal organizations like the Nazi *Sicherheitsdienst* to which Zig-Zag had belonged.

Sadly but predictably, Zig-Zag became a typical déclassé immigrant from central Europe. His extensive German legal training and knowledge of Prussian government regulations mattered not one whit on American soil, and at the age of forty-three, he took a permanent job with Sears and Roebuck in New Jersey selling carpets. In his early years in the United States, I sent him money, diplomatically labeled as loans, for outright gifts would have offended him. We corresponded until his death in 1990. No one ever memorialized Zig-Zag's brilliant and heroic service. In fact, his widow, a German national whom he married in Kassel, never knew what Zig-Zag had done in Berlin until I told her and their son. "I always knew how much he respected you," she said. "This helps explain why."

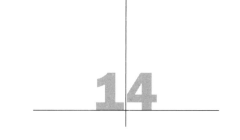

A NARROW ESCAPE

LESS THAN TWO MONTHS AFTER I ARRIVED IN BERLIN, THE SOVIET intelligence defector Vladimir came into my life. You'll recall from the introduction that the U.S. Army's G-2 had turned him over to me when he said he wished to defect from the NKVD. SSU-X-2 had decided to move him to Frankfurt-am-Main in the American zone for safer interrogation. Because heavy fog had closed the Tempelhof airport indefinitely, I decided to drive him—accompanied by two burly sergeants—through the Soviet zone to Frankfurt. Ever so gingerly, I edged my car toward the armed guards at the entrance to the Soviet zone outside Berlin. After I gave them cigarettes, they saluted me and elevated the giant pole barrier blocking passage from Berlin to the autobahn and the West.

The trip down the autobahn through the Soviet zone was a long one. I was driving a small, air-cooled, Czechoslovakian-built Tatra capable of 110 miles per hour, a phenomenal speed back then. My boss at the time, Lawrence de Neufville, had taken the car from its former owner, a dead SS major general,[1] and later turned it over to me. The sight of numerous Russian military vehicles alongside the autobahn made us nervous. In order not to draw additional attention to our conspicuous vehicle, I made sure I maintained the speed of traffic.

The trip, just over a hundred miles, seemed to last forever. Finally, we came to Helmstedt and slowed down before the huge pine, painted with red and white stripes, that blocked our passage. A small Russian private, Tommy gun slung across his shoulders, ambled up to our car. We had the radio blaring, and our prisoner was chewing some gum we'd given him. *"Russki dokument?"* he said, and we answered, *"Ja, wir haben sie hier."* Yes, we have them here.

Once across the border, we refueled at a British petrol station. Gale-force winds were blowing and, while a *Wehrmacht* prisoner loaded us up from ice-cold Afrika Korps gas cans, they threatened to carry off the car's raised hood.

The autobahn ended in Helmstedt. We played with the maps, searching for the best route south through the Harz Mountains to Kassel in the state of Hesse, but soon we became hopelessly lost. There were few road signs in the Harz Mountains, and most just pointed to the next hamlet down the road.

Only ten miles inside the British zone, the Tatra suddenly sputtered, went into a skid across the highway, and died. Soon the inevitable group of European gamins gathered in the rain. English lorries piled up. With all this manpower, we soon turned the car around, but it wouldn't start, and so off we headed to the English officers' club for help. There, two captains placidly sipped their tea and explained where the garage was, without offering the use of a phone. Miffed, we went plowing on foot through the mud and a half a mile later came upon a garage at a British ordnance company, part of a British division that had fought at El Alamein in Africa.

The British sergeant was most courteous. He promised to go back to the Tatra and tow it into his garage using the only vehicle he had, a fifteen-and-a-half-ton tank retriever, about the largest thing on wheels I had ever seen. Cruising through the medieval town where the garage was located, we felt as out of place as if we had been riding the Santa Fe Superchief through Boston.

"This Tatra is a rather odd European car," I said to the British sergeant once we were at the garage. "Do you know it?"

"Yes, sir."

"I only mention it because we had trouble with the fuel line earlier."

"Not to worry," he said and proceeded briskly to the front of the car, lifted the hood, and prepared to work on the engine, not knowing that it was situated in the back of this peculiar auto. An Englishmen never shows embarrassment—he made as if he were interested in the battery and only later tended to the engine in the rear.

My turn for embarrassment came later. After two or three English mechanics had played with the carburetor, taken the fuel pump apart, and tested the fuel lines, it suddenly dawned on me that Sergeant O'Brien, who had replaced me as driver after we left the Soviet zone, might have accidentally hit the Tatra's secret gas switch near the foot brakes. That was it. Too cold to be red in the face, we apologized profusely and passed out cigarettes and cigars to all, which we had brought along in case the Soviet border guards demanded them.

We didn't have time to contemplate what would have happened had I hit the secret gas switch inside the Soviet zone. Running late by now, we traveled down to the town of Bad Harzburg with its half-timbered, orange-tiled buildings, then began a long, steep ascent, changing gears from fourth to third to second. Losing power, we were finally forced into first gear, limping along at ten miles an hour. Although still daytime, it was dark, and the rain had turned to snow flurries. There was no ordnance depot for another forty miles.

I recalled an incident from my childhood where my father had driven me to Maine to see a solar eclipse and a new house he had designed at Bar Harbor. We traveled up and down the New England hills in an air-cooled Franklin. Air-cooled engines, he said, tended to "freeze" when climbing long hills. The remedy was to stop and let the engine cool twenty minutes. Suddenly recalling this, I announced with false confidence the source of our problem and its cure. By now, smoke was pouring from the streamlined fin over the engine. We didn't dare stop while we had any momentum on such a steep hill, but with each grinding mile we grew more anxious. Finally, we reached a plateau some four thousand feet above sea level. The wind screeched through the dark pines. Guenther, O'Brien, and I piled out, pulled up the tail fin, and prayed. As sparks and smoke sputtered from the eight overheated cylinders, we poured in four gallons of oil and twelve of gas. O'Brien took the "Jerry" cans, Guenther held the hood against the wind, and I adjusted the sieve.

After we climbed back in the car, the engine started easily, but our problems hadn't ended. As we drove down the tortuous mountain road, the snow turned to sleet. The windshield wiper was useless, and by now, so were the brakes. We limped along the road toward Göttingen and, despite our slow speed, nearly killed a horse pulling a cart. Approaching Kassel we discovered that the bridge was out, then became lost on the detour.

Finally, we arrived on the outskirts of heavily bombed Kassel, at which point we realized we couldn't reach Frankfurt by nightfall. In Kassel I called the CIC for help, wondering what to say—that we were transporting a Soviet defector? They might not keep the secret. Instead, I told them we had a captive German implicated in the concentration camp atrocities. The CIC quickly interpreted this to mean that he was Martin Bormann, Hitler's missing adjutant, and spread the word. Within minutes, eight

CIC personnel materialized and escorted us to lavish quarters for the night.

The "prisoner" couldn't be kept in jail, so O'Brien was chosen to guard him in a makeshift security pen. Our ruse worked. In the morning we delivered Vladimir to his future interrogators in Frankfurt; then I went on to SSU headquarters in Wiesbaden to report the delivery of our first NKVD defector. We all recognized that this mission could result in a treasure trove of information about the Soviets.

On the trip back we had a narrow escape. My companion knew Russian, and as we scooted along the autobahn toward Berlin, he read the signs, one of which said, "Glory to Stalin, Berlin 175 kilometers." By and by we approached the dreaded autobahn exits to Berlin. Too many Americans and British, we knew, had missed the exit to the Western-occupied sectors of the city and to their sorrow ended up in Soviet hands. We spotted a small sign in English, "Hq., Berlin District," with an arrow pointing right.

"Should we go right?" I asked the driver.

"No, the Russian sign in the center says, " 'Berlin, straight ahead.' "

So we went straight. Then it occurred to me that this must be the damned devilish exit we had been warned about. We were taking the route through Potsdam, sacred Kremlin of the Russian sector, and that meant trouble. The other side of the four-lane autobahn was lost in dark fog. We reversed course and, coming back on the wrong side of the road, found the correct turnoff, but not until a Soviet guard with a Tommy gun accosted us. "You'll cause accidents driving on the wrong side of the road," he screamed in Russian, demanding two packages of cigarettes before we continued. Carrying some liquor in the back that we didn't want him to see lest he confiscate it, we rocketed off and took the correct exit, at last bringing an end to our harrowing trek.[2]

Three weeks later, Wiesbaden reported that the interrogation of Vladimir had progressed along with his medical treatment for drug addiction. Then, he escaped. We never found out whether he had been a plant all along, or a genuine defector who changed his mind after possible mishandling by overly harsh interrogators. At any rate, Vladimir didn't end up being the treasure trove of information we had hoped for.

Defections worked both ways, of course. Those from Soviet intelligence were rare, but extremely helpful. In 1947 the Berlin station recruited the head of the Soviet intelligence registry in Berlin, one Captain Rebrov, as an agent in place. He supplied originals of all messages between Berlin and the NKVD in Moscow, so many that the Berlin station's translators couldn't keep up with them all. He simply removed the original from the registry and falsely noted that it had been sent to Moscow. He craftily reasoned that if anyone asked Moscow where the message was, Moscow would say they couldn't find it, and no one would be surprised since the Moscow filing system was so bad that documents frequently could not be found. When Rebrov's nerves broke, my successor in Berlin, Tom Polgar, drove him out of the Soviet sector to safety in the American sector of Berlin.[3] Rebrov later moved to the United States where he taught army officers about Russia.

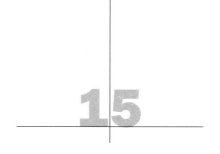

THE JOE HOUSE

The whirlwind investigating, wooing, and transporting of our first NKVD defector four hundred miles to Frankfurt caused me to fall behind in other duties, and on my return to Berlin I threw myself into work. My colleagues and I spent hours reading voluminous intelligence summaries from various agencies, conferring, analyzing agents' information, and firing off reports to Wiesbaden and Washington. At night we debriefed and instructed agents, often for hours at a time, at secluded spots far away from the office.

We were woefully understaffed for our responsibilities. One cause was the drastically lower SSU budget set by Truman, who was probably still unaware of the extent of the Soviet menace. The other was the too-rapid demobilization of many of the U.S. Army's best officers. Talented linguists went home, while less able officers chose to remain. Such indiscriminate redeployment crippled U.S. intelligence agencies, and it was galling.[1] The more experienced British handled redeployment better. They retained officers with military government skills for an extra year's service and offered enticing seven-year contracts to attract better men to help govern Germany.[2]

Nathaniel Batchelder, former headmaster of my prep school, Loomis, wrote my mother,

> We Americans boast of being practical people. . . . We are bringing boys home from all fronts without regard to the consequences. . . . When we talk about compulsory service, we talk about a year. As far as occupation goes, a year is no good. You simply can't train a boy, send him overseas, use him effectively, and bring him home in twelve months. Moreover, we shouldn't use the eighteen- and nineteen-year-olds in the occupation

forces. We need people of reasonable maturity who understand that they are not merely police but ambassadors. Well, I'm glad there are some like Dick who are willing to stay.[3]

SSU shared my frustration, and in November asked the War Department for permission to convert us from officers to better-paid civilians so that we would be more likely to stay on past our army discharge dates. In December I was offered the choice between becoming a captain or a civilian, provided I agreed to stay an additional six months beyond the time when I would have been eligible for discharge from the Army. It was a difficult decision. In dealing with the Germans, being military was most helpful. A lieutenant was more impressive to them than a better-paid civilian. On the other hand, in dealing with West Pointers, it was more advantageous to be a civilian than a lieutenant. I opted for the civilian status, but the Army promoted me to captain in April before my formal discharge.

I continued to dream about becoming a reporter, but Walter Kerr, the *New York Herald Tribune* correspondent who had recently been based in Moscow, cautioned me that newspapers "hire for Europe only from their New York offices. They find it easier to make a linguist than a reporter." Gradually, my increasing fascination with espionage pushed the thought of reporting and other careers into the background. My boss at the Wall Street law firm, J. Edward Lumbard Jr., suggested that I return home as soon as allowed or abandon the law.

It was while mulling over these possibilities that I was moved into the Joe house, where I would remain for the rest of my time in Berlin. As the months went by, my German rapidly improved, thanks in part to bilingual maids who unfailingly followed my instruction: "Speak to me only in German unless the house is on fire." They took pride in my progress and brought me the daily *Telegraf* to read each morning.

The Joe house was a warm oasis in the middle of a grim, collapsed city. I moved from a solitary existence in a shattered house lacking heat and hot water into a smoothly run, warm inn with a fascinating variety of dinner guests. I gave a glowing account of the new accommodations to my mother, in part because she had expressed concern about my living conditions as winter approached:

> I live in a house with a big radio, hot water, and heat. I am even sleeping between sheets for the first time in five months. Besides a fairly good cook,

we have five maids and a handyman in this house (paid for by the German people). They do everything except read my mail and write letters. . . . When [my car] doesn't start in the morning, all the gals file out and push it down the drive.

The SSU agents staying in the Joe House were a diverse mixture. A businessman from Dresden stood out with his guttural Saxon accent, farther from the Prussian German I heard in Berlin than an Alabama accent is from that of New England. There was a Catholic bishop, a German Social Democratic politician, and most interesting of all, a former *Luftwaffe* major, one of Germany's new jet pilots. This was the German Rhodes scholar with the skewed ideas about German history, whom I mentioned earlier. Now, according to his SI officer, he was busy identifying what the Soviet Army was up to as it disassembled jets and jet factories, loaded the parts onto trains, and carted them off to the Soviet Union. The dashing pilot had been shot down over England and imprisoned in Canada, where he escaped. Speaking flawless English and dressed in civilian clothes, he had traveled through the United States, made his way to Argentina, and there caught a boat back to Europe, where he rejoined the *Luftwaffe* and flew against Russia. As if this portrait weren't intriguing enough, he was permitted to bring his sensual blonde mistress to live with us. In my sheltered life I had never seen two persons of the opposite sex share quarters unless they were married.

The intellectual talk flowed in our Joe house drawing room over cognac and coffee. The agents, between their furtive stints under Soviet occupation, were starved for free-flowing conversation, not to mention curious about me as a young, educated, and well-traveled American, a breed most of them hadn't encountered before. We conversed about prewar Germany, the Nazis, England, and most of all about the threatening Soviet Union and America's attitude toward it. I admired their courage in risking their lives to lift the Soviet yoke from their country's shoulders. They appreciated my zest for dialogue and intense interest in history and geopolitics.

I didn't know that many of these agents would be captured by the Soviets in the fall of 1946. In 1993 I learned that the SI operations in 1945 and 1946 were, in the opinion of a CIA officer who later served in Berlin, so loose that the Soviets easily "rolled up" networks in their zone, capturing many agents and throwing them into Siberian prisons, where they would stagnate until released in 1955. I never found out whether the colorful pilot was among those imprisoned, although I suspect he was. When the agents returned from Siberia, the CIA offered them financial compensation for their suffering.[4]

Strangely, according to my recollection, neither Washington, Wiesbaden, nor the head of SSU in Berlin ever asked X-2 to vet SI spies operating out of Berlin, even though I had been asked to perform that role vigorously in London and again at Wiesbaden.[5] All I recall of laxness, other than my not being asked to vet agents (which was probably not the cause of their undoing), was one example of poor recruitment that was quickly corrected. An athletic Congressional Medal of Honor winner joined SI briefly in Berlin. His superiors quickly observed that his courage on the battlefield stemmed from a degree of recklessness not acceptable on spy missions and sent him packing as a security risk. In tribute to his wartime heroism, however, they didn't tell him that he had flunked out. I was told he had been close to blowing our operations. Whether he had anything to do with our agents getting rolled up, I don't know.

In any event, the tug-of-war between Soviet and American intelligence was definitely heating up in Berlin. It was clear by now that we were engaged in a new war, the Cold War. What wasn't clear was that this was just the beginning of nearly five decades of high-stakes tension between the Soviet Union and the United States.

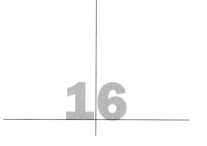

PLUMBING THE
RUSSIAN MIND

AWAY FROM THE CONGENIAL, RELAXED ATMOSPHERE AT THE JOE house, our counterespionage efforts against the Soviets intensified. Zig-Zag's intermittent roundup of Soviet agents was overshadowed by our opponent's far more numerous and aggressive actions, such as tossing former *Abwehr* officers who might be sympathetic to the United States into jail for extended periods. The Communist party's slogan was, the end justifies the means. That attitude resulted in daily Soviet efforts to domi-nate Berlin, often by thin subterfuge. The Russians regarded the city as their hard-earned prize. They merely tolerated the Western occupying forces there; we were a diplomatic necessity that Stalin had intended to undermine from the start.[1]

SSU cables and reports from Berlin in the winter of 1945 to 1946, some written by me and others under my supervision, reflected the Soviets' paranoid suspicion of the West. On January 25, our headquarters in Wies-baden reported that an NKVD translator had been imprisoned because his mistress, although a Communist sympathizer, had worked at the American embassy before the war. A Russian general explained to our double agent that he could not release the translator because of his sub-versive connection with the Americans.[2] On February 20, I called Wash-ington's attention to a *News of the World* report from London that the Russians, sometimes disguised as German police, were arresting German judges and officials living in the British and American sectors of Berlin. The British protested to the Allied *Kommandatura*, whereupon the Rus-sians gave evasive answers. We filed repeated reports concerning NKVD espionage agents operating almost openly in the American and British sectors, seeking to learn what the western Allies were doing.

This wasn't the worst of it. Russians dressed in civilian clothes had been robbing passengers arriving at railroad stations. German police raids came up empty-handed because Soviet agents inside the police tipped off the robbers ahead of time.

On April 3, 1946, one of our now slightly expanded X-2 staff relayed to SSU-Wiesbaden a British MI-6 analysis of NKVD organizational structure in Berlin. It revealed that there were four distinct operational groups reporting to a Soviet major general and, more succinctly, that "the peculiar feature is . . . the intimate control exercised by the NKVD over the police. In Berlin this control is exercised in conjunction with the KPD [Communist Party] over the entire police system, including the police in the Allied sectors."[3] The author commented,

[M]uch of the original material came from our British counterparts in Berlin, whose general technique is the cautious exploitation of informants and occasional disaffection of Soviet agents who are evacuated to a safer spot (in the British zone near the Rhine) for lengthy interrogation. Much of the British information . . . corroborates that obtained by us through our principal means: double-agents. In view of the demonstrable superiority of British information on order of battle obtained largely through disaffection, we may henceforth direct our efforts in that direction. . . . [T]he full exploitation of disaffection hinges upon the skill and thoroughness of the subsequent interrogation. . . . Here, our British counterpart is in an advantageous position, being able, with certainty, to call upon the services of a staff of expert interrogators, well versed in the subject matter, alert, industrious, and trained to write interrogation reports.

The report puzzled over why Captain Skurin, who seemed a superior opponent, was a member of the NKVD, rather than some supposed higher-level Soviet intelligence agency. Was the NKVD a cover to make him appear less important than he was? We noted,

Captain Skurin is definitely in the high-grade espionage bracket, and both the quality of some of his agents and the kind of tasks he commits to them place him beyond the pale of the ordinary NKVD officer. His last instructions to SAVOY [Hans Kemritz] to gather economic intelligence of a specific kind could by no stretch of the imagination be brought under the heading of counterintelligence operations. Our knowledge of the internal nature of the NKVD structure would be appreciably expanded if we could determine Skurin's exact status within the framework of the Russian secret service.

On April 22, my X-2 superior at Wiesbaden, Sidney Lennington, threw cold water on the suggestion that we arrange for the defection of a secretary to the Russian secret service named Doccia. He wrote to me,

> Were Doccia in a really important position where she could give us information of greater range and of definitive exploitation possibilities, then the project would be encouraged . . . but I would very much appreciate your views on the advisability of defection with the subsequent transferal and disposal of the body which would present quite a problem and which, on the basis of expected results localized in nature, would not justify action.[4]

He was referring to the practice of relocating defectors and getting them jobs to protect them against Soviet retaliation—a big task and one not to be undertaken lightly.

Humdrum reports like these about low-level Soviet intelligence efforts occupied much of our time. We recognized we were outnumbered, that the Russians had hostile intentions, and that we should better utilize our limited resources. We had to concentrate on the highest-level intelligence operations, if we could identify them, and let many of the rest go. Was there not a smarter, quicker tactic for identifying top-level Soviet operators than relying on Zig-Zag's excellent efforts to penetrate Soviet intelligence through former *Abwehr* agents whom the Russians had recruited? While these low-level cat-and-mouse games played out, I sought out opportunities, especially while pursuing my Sunday hobby of filming, to meet Russians and learn whether individually they were as hostile as we knew their government to be. It was much harder to get into the minds of Russians than Germans. There were two enormous barriers: our inability to speak to each other in anything but broken or, at best, passable German, and the Russians' clear fear of being open with us when their dreaded government—under Stalin's iron fist—had ordered them to avoid and distrust all capitalists. The average Russian soldier was a peasant. He had next to no education and little conception of the outside world. If he liked America, it was because the United States, in his mind, was proletarian.

Occasionally when my companions and I ventured through the Soviet sector, Russian soldiers would wave us down, asking for a ride. We always obliged. Communication consisted of German (a third of Russian officers spoke German) or "Russki-Americanski" sign language. One day I had this conversation:

"Can you take me to Warschau Bahnhof? I have to catch the train for Frankfurt-an-der-Oder."

"Yes, climb in."

"Willys no good for Russian Army, but good for American Army."

"You mean this jeep?

"No, this Willys we are riding in."

"Where do you live in Russia?"

"Gorki."

"How long have you been in the Red Army?"

"Seven years."

"That's a nice fur cap you have."

"Yes."

"Would you like to buy a watch?"

"No, I have three now."

"What will you do with the watches?"

"I shall buy a farm with each one in Russia. I get out here. Thank you."

That same day three drunken Russian officers, waving a bottle of cognac, stopped our jeep.

"Potsdam," they said.

"Potsdamer Platz or Potsdam the city?"

"Eh."

"Do you mean Potsdam way away or Potsdam very very close?" I pulled out a map and showed them both places.

"*Viel Geld und viel Vodka*," one Russian said, trying to entice us to take him fifteen miles to Potsdam. Having no intention of going that far, we offered them a ride to Zehlendorf, our destination, but they didn't seem to understand. On arrival at Zehlendorf, we tried to push them out of the jeep. They wouldn't budge; they just sat there waving ten-dollar bills and vodka bottles. They continued talking, with much smiling and backslapping:

"Roosevelt, good. Churchill, no good. Truman, no good. American Poles, bad. Russian Poles, good. Dardenelles Russian. What are you?"

"A capitalist from Wall Street."

They were shocked. How could I be a capitalist? I was a first lieutenant driving a jeep—therefore I was a worker and good. It was enough to uproot them from their seats.

Another day I met a Russian Air Force lieutenant in Alexander Platz, which resembled Columbus Circle in New York, except it was in the slums. It had been a Communist Party hub before 1933, and in 1945 was near the Russian Army headquarters. The black market thrived at Alexander Platz. I went there to take photographs from the center of the circle, safe from the raiding police. A Russian lieutenant addressed me in German:

"You are in the American Air Force, *nicht?*"

When I said yes, we chatted about little things and nothing, and then he asked me if I had any penicillin. No, I replied. Perhaps he knew where I could buy a Leica? (Leica cameras, the world's finest, were manufactured in the Soviet zone.) No, he didn't. Where did he live? East of Gorki. Where did I live? New York. The Russian Air Force had bombed Berlin to ruins, no? I had rather thought the British and Americans had done most of the bombing, the Soviets most of the shelling. He and his five comrades, who used him as an interpreter, explained that they did not like Poland, did like America, didn't like the English. Curious about them, I asked them what they wanted most to have in the world. Girls, slippers, and dresses, but first, penicillin. One of them expressed his opinion of the Allies' relative war effort: England was a thumb, America the big finger, and Russia all five fingers.

Another day, accompanied by a friend, I was photographing water scenes along the Berliner Spree, reminiscent of the Thames, but narrower. As I reached the end of the pier, three Russian officers and a civilian woman approached me. The senior officer, who must have been in his early thirties, wore an immaculate covert-cloth uniform and smart boots and carried himself with dignity. Two large gold stars on his gold epaulets caught our attention, and I saluted. As we passed by I took his photograph. Turning around, he asked, "Does one of you speak German?"

"Yes, a little," I answered.

"Do you like Berlin?"

"Yes."

"How long have you been in the American Army?

"Only three years."

"Where do you live in America?"

"New York."

"It is a very large prosperous city, isn't it—seven million and a half people?"

"Yes, sir. Tell me, are you in the navy?"

"No, I am in the army. I must go now, our party is late."

He also asked, out of the hearing of his companions, whether New York City had the tallest buildings in the world. I had heard from a Cornish fisherman in England that *Pravda*, the leading Soviet newspaper, had claimed that Moscow planned to build the world's tallest building. This Russian officer was as polite and distinguished looking a gentleman as I had met in any army. Later, I learned he was a Russian lieutenant general.

In December I drove to the Anhalter Bahnhof where there were always Red Army men awaiting trains for Leipzig, Dresden, and Breslau. I was walking away from my parked jeep when suddenly the horn erupted. Turning, I saw a Russian captain, his face wreathed in smiles, standing by my vehicle, his hand holding the horn down. A young Russian lieutenant in his group explained that the captain wanted a ride some five hundred meters.

"Do you mean five hundred kilometers?" I asked, smiling. "I know you Russians—you always want long rides."

"No, comrade, only five hundred meters."

I believed him, so off we went. Down the street we came to his billet in a dilapidated building. He dove into the ruins, and reappeared with two Germans carrying luggage. Soon there were eight suitcases and more miscellaneous bundles standing by the jeep. The Russians were as happy as children at a birthday party. "Now we travel back to the station." They loaded the jeep, all the while observing that the Americans were good, the English no good. I told them they could walk to the station, as their luggage had filled up the jeep. They refused in the usual Russian fashion, with big smiles, then piled onto the jeep like Keystone cops—four in the front seat, three on the hood.

Back at the station we exchanged cigarettes and made small talk. The lieutenant said that since he and I were the same rank, we were friends and needn't talk with the three captains in the group. Everyone laughed. We must drink, he said—only thirty minutes remained before the train departed.

We could go to a restaurant, he added. So once again we piled into the jeep, this time seven of us. The "restaurant" turned out to be his billet. An old German couple lived there in a wet cellar. They pulled out some firewater strong enough to warm the North Pole. I knew it was bad manners to mix water with the drink, but I wanted to drive home without unsolicited incidents. The Russians protested volubly, but, uncharacteristically, I should add, permitted me to dilute the stuff. One officer, otherwise refined in appearance and speech, let his drink dribble all over his clean winter coat until it was soaked.

They served me a pint and, out of courtesy, throwing away my good intentions, I drank the whole thing. It took eight hours for the buzz to fade away, and I wasted an hour trying to find my way back to the Joe house from Kurfurstendamm.

My overall impression of the Russians was that, at least as individuals, they were trying to understand Americans. No Frenchman, or Englishman, or German was as convivial as a Russian. However boorish, uneducated, or lacking in table manners (the Germans harped on these "deficiencies" as if the world were built on such slender considerations), they struck me as a lusty, direct, self-reliant, friendly people.

Later that evening I attended a party given by Barbara Güttler and her mother and the talk turned to the Russians. One guest from East Berlin reported, "You know, Frank is in the hospital with a broken rib."

"What happened?" another guest asked.

"Those damned Russians."

"What?"

"They stole his bike from him Wednesday, and when he resisted, they kicked him, breaking his rib."

All the Germans turned to me, as if that proved the point they'd been hammering away at for weeks: that the Russians were uncivilized, Asiatic brutes bent on ruling Deutschland with an undisciplined iron hand.

"You know," I said, "if I speak to you about concentration camps, you say there are good and bad Germans. Perhaps there are also good Russians as well as bad."

"You are always sticking up for the Russians, Lieutenant. You are the only American officer who has never criticized them."

"Stories such as you have told build the hatred that starts wars."

"Yes, but there is no point to your denying that they are bad."

"Unless people make efforts to understand one another, how can there be peace in the world? Are you aware, or have you forgotten, what happened in Kharkov, Kiev, Odessa, Novgorod, where SS troops slaughtered civilians?

"Two wrongs don't make a right."

On Christmas morning at a train station in the American sector, I was taking motion pictures of American and Russian soldiers standing by. A Russian approached and began thumping his chest. Thinking he wanted his picture taken, I zoomed over to him. He waved the smaller Russian soldiers back, then grew distraught. He was a major, I noted. The others were privates. Then it dawned on me: he was leading his flock of twenty ragged soldiers to the train and didn't want pictures taken. We let him have his way, and soon a better filming opportunity arose as a three-wheel vehicle approached with ten Russians clinging to it. It was a perfect movie shot, so I ground away. Two of them shook their fists at me, but this time I ignored them, not willing to give up my Sunday hobby. The Russians' pervasive fear of being photographed reflected the Soviet paranoia about secrecy—the photographer was probably an American spy. If an individual Russian did not share that fear, he certainly did not relish the punishment he would receive if observed by the NKVD violating orders not to permit his photograph to be taken.

Seeking out Russians, I longed to talk with someone who would discuss politics in a sustained, quiet manner—preferably in English! I appealed to one Pushkin, a Russian-born U.S. Army interpreter at the Four-Power Allied Council (*Kommandatura*) who in late October had verified that our prized NKVD "defector," Vladimir, was truly Russian and not a German imposter. Pushkin agreed to introduce me to a worldlier Russian.

"Come over Sunday, we're having a little party for the Russian liaison sections," he said.

It was crowded, and I ended up standing next to a Russian lieutenant.

"I see you are the only American here who is not from the liaison section," he said, breaking the ice.

"Right."

"Then you do not speak Russian?"

"Only *yellow bluttey bar*," I replied, phonetic for I love you. (Laughter.) "But your English is excellent. Do you speak other foreign languages as well?"

"Yes, Spanish."

"That's unusual for a Russian, isn't it?

"Not exactly."

"I mean, you're not a neighbor of Spain. It would seem more natural to learn German, French, English, Italian, first."

"Perhaps."

This closed the conversation, and I soon joined a group dancing. Later, I listened while a General Staff major engaged the same Russian in some friendly, but earnest questions:

"I am one of those Americans who regrets the loose talk you hear about our nations going to war," he said. "It's rubbish, but we do know too little about each other, and for that reason I'm anxious to ask you some questions. Are you, for example, a member of the Communist Party?"

"I do not think I understand."

"I mean, you have an important position as liaison officer for General Smirnoff and the Americans. Did you have to be a member of the Communist Party for such a trusted position?"

"I do not know, but I have always been a member of the party."

"Are you a professional soldier, or did you have a civilian career?"

"No, I am, how do you say? An all-time soldier."

"In Russia, how much does the party count? If you have two good doctors and one is in the party and the other is not, which one obtains the desirable state post?"

"The Communist. You see, it is considered that the members of the party think more of the general welfare than someone who has no more talent for the same job."

"Do you think Russia will ever have political liberty in the same sense in which the Western powers understand it?"

"Yes, we do."

"Could you tell us how public officials are selected?"

"Gladly. We have workers' committees in the factories, committees for the collective farms, and of course, Party committees for the small towns as an entity. In proposing a candidate for these groups, they know which men are well known to the people for their good deeds or war bravery. A man who has not remained popular or become a skilled workman may be—how do you say?—weeded out. There are many arguments about the candidates. The best men win."

An American captain approached our little group. "Tell me, will Stalin ever allow an opposition party in Russia?" he asked.

"Look at it this way. What do you think the Conservatives in Britain would do if they won ninety-five percent of the votes?" he asked, implying that they would eliminate the small opposition as superfluous.

"During the war," the American captain countered, "the *Chicago Tribune* printed articles that amounted to praise for Nazi principles. We—the vast majority—didn't agree with this silliness, but we tolerated it because freedom of the press makes for a better government in the long run."

"Yes, but the *Chicago Tribune* was a fascist paper and was not good for America."

At this point Pushkin walked up and insisted that the questioning stop. Privately, he explained that this Russian officer had been invaluable to the American military government by persuading his superior to better understand American positions. We must not risk offending him by a long tiring session. We understood, and reluctantly went back to dancing and watching our drunken colleagues knock the mistletoe from the chandelier.

CIVILIAN STATUS

In January 1946 SSU permitted me to wear civilian clothes whenever it would assist in my work, believing that apparent civilian status would enable me to present SSU matters more strongly to colonels who often refused to discuss matters with a first lieutenant. (Months later I was made a captain and soon thereafter discharged from the army to assume a civil service rank equivalent to the rank of lieutenant colonel.) Although civvies accomplished wonders, this progress was hindered at the beginning of February when various crises began overtaxing our small staff. My three phones rang constantly. Sometimes a major might wait two hours to see me for five minutes. My appointments stretched out ten days in advance, and nearly every evening was devoted to work.

By the middle of February SSU began adding personnel. It was easy to recruit for Berlin, which was rapidly becoming recognized as the espionage capitol of the world. Wilma Taber, who had succeeded me as vetting officer in Wiesbaden, asked her bosses to let her come work as my assistant. Instead, the job went to Barnard graduate Rosemary, whose last name I omit for reasons which will become apparent shortly. She and other new staff soon helped lessen the workload, and by the end of February things were going smoothly. For the first time in eight weeks, I almost got to the bottom of my in-box.

Rosemary was unique. Having grown up in Egypt as the child of American missionaries, she had an easy sophistication. After being transferred from OSS to the Nuremberg trial staff, she became infatuated with a British MI-6 officer. When he was transferred to Berlin, she managed to follow him, although she had neither a job in the city, nor documents entitling her to be there. After a while, in probable need of income and legalized status, she obtained a job with SSU as my assistant. She was living with the MI-6 officer, whose wife remained in England, causing two fortyish maiden secretaries to protest that this "scandalous" relationship imperiled SSU security. After that, we arranged for Rosemary to live in a dorm housing other SSU women.

That winter, the situation in the Joe house changed abruptly. The luxury we enjoyed didn't escape the notice of cold, malnourished Berlin residents. With Germans going hungry, it didn't help to have American GIs in the house throwing food around. This was exacerbated by the fact that the American supply sergeant was careless enough to make love to two of the German housemaids. Not surprisingly, morale broke down, and the servants started stealing food. In addition to the pilfering, they began ratting on each other to me. Although a reluctant personnel manager, I felt it necessary to order the maids' houses searched, their personal possessions inventoried, and the mansion reinventoried. Then I gave them twenty-four hours to restore what they had taken.

If that was not enough, thieves removed tires from my car three times, and Russians for a second time scared the maids. One day two Russian officers pounded on the door when I was out, boorishly demanding entrance. A maid refused to let them in, fearing robbery or worse, and fortunately the Russians left, but I had to go through another long cross-examination of my servants, make traces of the Russian footprints, and search the garden, heavily armed, to see if anything was untoward. By now I was armed all the time. I wore one weapon showing, for psychological effect, and another concealed.

By late February, my staff and I were worn out. No activity is more exciting, or nerve-wracking, than spying. Our agents were in great danger, and we identified with them, worrying when they had close scrapes or weren't heard from. Our work was so secret, we couldn't let off steam by discussing it with army personnel, who enjoyed calm, part-time duty while awaiting redeployment back home.

I applied for leave to ski in Switzerland, preferring to ski there than in the Bavarian Alps, where the show was too solidly army. The Swiss hotelkeepers, having sat out the war, coveted long-absent tourist income and particularly warmed to the prospect of American GIs lavishly spending their hard currency. Centuries-old Swiss neutrality required that no foreign troops enter their country, but the GIs had no civilian clothes, and so the Swiss yen for dollars won out.[1] Thus, Americans were allowed to visit Switzerland in full military uniform (I was still technically in the army—though wearing civilian clothes in Berlin), but only for one week.

My office sought an extension for me; when it was refused, I was ordered to go on to Paris for an additional week. They, too, wanted me to benefit from extended time away.

The U.S. Army sought to boost morale by arranging low-cost package tours to Switzerland. Taking advantage of this, on March 3 I boarded a train in Berlin, changed to a tour bus in Frankfurt, and was soon zipping along on an electric train through tortuous valleys and tunnels to San Moritz, one of Switzerland's famed ski resorts. I rented skis and took the cable car up Mt. Corviglia, not far from Lake Como in northern Italy. The Alps glistened under fresh powdery snow, and the long runs were a delight, although I hadn't skied since accidentally turning a cartwheel in a downhill race in Vermont three years earlier, and I was a trifle rusty.

On the slopes I met an anti-Communist White Russian who had fled the Soviet Union. As we skied and chatted, I wondered if he were a Soviet plant assigned to snuggle up to me. SSU Bern dispatched an officer to watch over me—he shortly proved his worth.

On the third and last day, the sun was particularly bright. After spending the morning photographing the breathtaking scenery, I decided to make up for lost time by rushing down the slopes with my Russian friend. It was about 1 PM, and the scanty ski patrol had retreated to a hut for lunch.[2] The surface near the summit was pocked with sitzmarks left by novice skiers. All of a sudden the tip of my lead ski shot under a sitzmark's broken crust, pitching me forward. My right arm and left shoulder throbbed with pain.

"If you can wiggle your hand," my Russian friend volunteered, "nothing is broken."

All ten fingers moved, so we started down. With both arms limp from the fall, I couldn't slow my descent by turning on my skis, and as a result I took one fall after another, especially in the last two kilometers where the trail down resembled an icy bobsled run.

At the bottom of the hill, the ski patrol took one look at my swollen shoulder and wrist, cut my jacket off, and transported me to the hospital. The doctor diagnosed two green-stick fractures in the right arm and a dislocated left shoulder, explaining that the top tendon had been pulled partly off the collarbone. They put the first in a cast, the second in a sling, and didn't charge me a dime.

The next morning at San Moritz, my SSU watcher from Bern announced that Swiss doctors were no good. I should go to the American hospital in Paris. I thought he was a sissy, and that the Swiss must know all about ski surgery—after all, I was the fifty-second American casualty in what we all laughingly called the Battle of San Moritz. But he insisted, adding for good measure that no doubt the Swiss doctor had put the cast on too tight.

I journeyed to Paris and checked in with the SSU office; Anne Heyneger, my former assistant in Wiesbaden, had transferred there in January. Then, I went to the American hospital at Neuilly. The cast, as predicted, was too tight, and the doctor sawed it off to prevent gangrene.

Anne and her roommate were fully at home in Paris. They included me in previously arranged visits to the opera and theater, to which we traveled by Metro. Like me, they preferred high-brow culture to the American movies then playing in Paris with French subtitles, movies like *The Wizard of Oz* and Orson Wells's *Citizen Kane*.[3] Feeling quite lofty, Anne and I attended *Lorenzaccio*, a heavy-going melodrama by Alfred de Musset about the assassination of Alexander de Medici.

Anne and her roommate invited me to accompany them to a cocktail party given by a Belgian friend, Robertine Lacquet, who lived in Neuilly with her parents. Robertine was a tall, dark-haired, attractive, and vivacious girl who spoke fluent English and German. We babbled away in three languages, having great fun. My ski injury stimulated her sympathy, and we dated several times. One night we danced cheek to cheek, her arms clasped around my sling. She joked about my having been wounded in the Battle of the Bulge. I learned she had been in Berlin in 1943 and my OSS antennae went up. What had she been doing there then? But I had sense enough not to ask. It might reveal she had been a Nazi sympathizer (not true, I later learned) and spoil a pleasant interlude.[4] We had so much fun that evening that I escorted her home, missed the Metro—with the fuel shortage, it stopped running at 11 PM—and had to walk several kilometers to my hotel near the Madeleine.

Robertine Lacquet stuck in my mind as someone who could be an interesting friend. When I returned to Berlin, we corresponded frequently. The ski injury that attracted her attention had been as worthwhile as the fresh Swiss air and the skiing.

After many months of cloudy skies and long nights, Berlin's spring began on April 1. Shrubs and flowers burst into bloom, a profusion of quince, forsythia, wisteria, cherry and apple blossoms, crocuses, tulips, and pansies. Faces turned more cheerful, especially on old women.

The change in weather had no effect on our spirits in the Joe house, however, where we were still on edge about the possibility of intruders. I rigged the garden lights so that I could switch them on from my second-floor bedroom whenever I heard a strange noise. One night I went out chasing imaginary burglars. The next night I stepped outside twice to see if some intruder had rung the doorbell. It turned out to be the shrill cry of a nightingale in the garden.

At this time right-wing supporters of Gen. Charles de Gaulle in the French Secret Service's Berlin office were asking SSU to exchange information with them, as we had done in London. De Gaulle had abruptly resigned in January as head of the interim French government, but he remained a political force. SSU officers knew one or two French intelligence officers in Berlin from the London era. We kept turning them down, suspecting that French Communists from the Resistance, who had joined the French Secret Service after France's liberation, would have access to anything we gave to the Gaullists.[5] Our hints to old colleagues on that point met with stiff denials. It occurred to me that Robertine, if willing to work in Berlin, might become a spy for us against the French Secret Service. She could verify or refute our fear that the Communists had rendered the French Secret Service an untrustworthy ally. Robertine said she had been in Berlin in 1943. Did that meant she harbored right-wing political tendencies, or at least had no sympathy for the Communists whose first loyalty clearly lay with Moscow? I didn't broach the subject until meeting her again in Paris in July.

Our after-dinner dialog at the Joe house was now enhanced by the gifted conversation of a new spy, "Gabriel," an alias I give her to protect her privacy. She had been sent to me by SSU-Wiesbaden. Her elf-like size was misleading. Gabriel had amazing power over others, especially men. A resourceful linguist who had worked for German intelligence during the war, she was also well read in history, philosophy, theater, and politics and, unlike many intellectuals, she was street smart. Gabriel was perfectly suited for counterespionage.

SSU-Wiesbaden instructed me to save Gabriel for a top-level assignment. My bosses emphasized she might become bored if idle. I was to keep her busy and well cared for until an appropriate assignment materialized. Accordingly, I paid special attention to her during dinner and afterwards in the drawing room, when the talk turned to geopolitics and German and European history. At first I was so awed by her knowledge and eloquence that, as she later remarked, I acted "severe and rigid."[6] Gradually, I relaxed, or else she maneuvered me into a more relaxed state.

She taught me how, in Germany at least, a man and woman encircle right arms before offering a toast.

Gabriel could take dictation in German, English, or French with equal ease. To keep her occupied, I asked her to compose a piece on Russian culture and history. It was thoughtful, solid, and objective. Gabriel had her reasons for helping the Americans. She judged them to be fairer to her country than the Russians, whom she greatly resented for their savage reparations, seizing of young men for forced labor in the USSR, and dictatorial administration of their zone of occupation outside Berlin.

Finding projects to keep an intellectual of her caliber busy was difficult. Partly in desperation and partly for selfish reasons, I conjured up a make-work project. Would she to like to type and retype my personal letters describing Berlin and the Russians? To pique her interest, I said they would be addressed not only to my family and closest friends, but also to the editor of the *Economist* in London, the author John Gunther, and my versatile congresswoman, Claire Boothe Luce, who was better known as a playwright and the wife of the publisher of *Time, Life,* and *Fortune.* Gabriel recognized all their names and rather liked helping export my political impressions of the Berlin scene to prominent opinion makers in Britain and the United States. She may have also thought this project would give her more insight into her future spymaster and influence how he presented Germany and the Russians to his bosses. So, I typed or dictated longer letters than usual, and she retyped them at the Joe house on my tiny portable Corona, which could put out four carbon copies, repeating the exercise six times so that thirty-five copies could be mailed out.

Those letters did far more than keep Gabriel occupied. One went to my old Yale Law School friend, Roy Steyer, who was serving on the prosecution staff for the Nuremberg trials. On learning that I was in Berlin, he suggested to a girl he was dating that she call on me when she traveled to Berlin on Nuremberg business. Her name was Elizabeth Fitzgerald.

One sunny day I was sitting in my majestic office in Dahlem overlooking a park-like stand of pine trees, musing that just a few years earlier, Field Marshall Keitel had sat in my chair, when the phone rang.

"Hello, are you Dick Cutler?"

"Yes."

"My name is Elizabeth Fitzgerald. I'm from Milwaukee and am just now in Berlin on an assignment for the Nuremberg trial. Roy Steyer is also there; he said he got a letter from you saying you were in Berlin. He knew I was coming up here for the weekend and suggested you might help me by arranging to get a jeep for me. He also said you might be able to advise me on the lay of the land. I'm to see a British admiral on business."

We arranged to have lunch. She was twenty-three, and an impressively smart Smith College graduate. OSS had recruited her for French translation in Washington and later transferred her to the Nuremberg trial staff as a reward for outstanding performance. Although not in the army, she wore the customary olive green uniform of civilians in the occupation forces. Her warm, quiet, serious demeanor made her stand out.

Liz Fitzgerald got her jeep, a map of Berlin, and traffic instructions on how to reach the admiral's office. Her assignment was to obtain documents in the British Admiralty's possession in Berlin proving that Alfred Rosenberg, a defendant in the Nuremberg trial, participated in an act of aggressive warfare by helping plan Hitler's invasion of neutral Norway in 1940. Rosenberg had been a notorious anti-Jewish propagandist. The prosecutors feared the court might not judge his written poison to be a criminal offense equal to that of giving orders to kill peaceful Norwegians. Liz obtained the documents, and in the end the court did convict Rosenberg, not just for helping plan the invasion of Norway, but also for participating in the extermination of Jews in the German-occupied part of the Soviet Union.[7]

With my enlarged staff, I felt less harassed and much more effective on the job. SSU now averaged fifteen officers and nine enlisted men, plus secretaries for a total of around thirty employees. Four or five worked directly for me in X-2, including the talented Tom Polgar, the hard-working Toivo Roswall, a native of Finland proficient in three or four languages, and Rosemary. Additional X-2 officers came back and forth from Wiesbaden on trouble-shooting missions. They included Sidney Lennington and Henry Hecksher. Sid was affable, witty, gentle, folksy, prematurely bald, and having been born in Brazil, the best American samba dancer in Germany. Henry, by contrast, was brilliant, intense, fearless, and genial, but sometimes impetuous. Formerly a judge in his native Hamburg, he knew the German mind and bureaucracy like the back of his hand.

My role as head of X-2 became progressively more important. Intoxicated by the increasing excitement and glamour, I started to consider resigning from the law firm and staying in the intelligence service. By July I had made up my mind—intelligence it would be—but I put off resigning from the firm until August, when I would travel to the United States on leave and break the news gently to my parents, whose hearts were set on my pursuing a legal career.

18

THE NUREMBERG TRIAL
AND A SOVIET
KIDNAPPING RING

As THE EXCITEMENT OF OUR COUNTERESPIONAGE WORK GREW, SO did our fascination with the dramatic proceedings at the Nuremberg war crimes trial. Throughout the winter of 1946 all of us in Berlin had been reading about the trial that had started in November 1945. The Allies had rounded up the top twenty-three Nazi officials remaining after Hitler, Himmler, and Goebbels committed suicide. Among the most prominent prisoners in the dock were Herman Göring, Admiral Karl Dönitz, who succeeded Hitler after his death, and Albert Speer, Hitler's architect and the head of war production.

The Allies accused the defendants of committing four crimes. One charge was violating established rules of warfare, such as the Geneva Convention's rules for treating prisoners of war. The other three crimes were arguably "new" and retroactive: crimes against peace, aggressive warfare in violation of treaties, and crimes against humanity. The last category included genocide and deportation, which in recent years has come to be known as "ethnic cleansing."

In Berlin we heard much about the trial of Admiral Dönitz. He started the war as the long-time chief of submarine, or U-boat, operations and later commanded the German Navy. Before committing suicide, Hitler appointed Dönitz as his successor. Dönitz, who spoke impeccable English, took the trial process seriously. Confidently and unevasively, he answered the prosecutor's questions in English rather than waiting for them to be translated from English into German.[1] His attitude made his testimony likely to be the most interesting of any defendant's. My curiosity aroused, I called Roy Steyer under an alias, Captain MacDonald, and arranged to visit the trial for the purpose of "educational recreation." Roy burst out laughing when he heard my alias. But this was no childish intelligence game. Our telephone lines ran through the Soviet zone, and we knew they were tapped.

The Nuremberg proceedings were impressive. Each morning the defendants were marched in from their cells to reserved seats. Behind the defendants twelve U.S. military police stood constant guard. The judges—American, British, Soviet, and French—sat behind a rostrum higher up in the courtroom. We spectators, after showing security passes, were ushered into a gallery looking down on the proceedings. The arm of each seat held a newly invented simultaneous translation device. Each spectator could rotate a dial to listen to his choice of four languages: German, English, French, or Russian. Questions and answers were simultaneously translated and spoken into the appropriate language channel. When I couldn't understand a German word on the "original" channel, I could switch quickly over to English and catch the translation of the word, then skip back to the original channel again. This dial system was the wonder of all who watched the trials. The French translators arranged it so that a woman translated the prosecutor's questions, a man, the defendant's. A listener could thereby easily identify whether the prosecution or defense was speaking.

The prisoners were as interesting as the trial itself. Balding Hermann Göring was ashen and lethargic from a long cold, his feet wrapped in an army blanket. Next to him sat Rudolf Hess, who had flown to Scotland early in the war—he claimed he was on a peace mission, but was arguably crazy—with his beetle-browed, sunken-eyed, haunted look. When he walked from the courtroom, it was with a stiff, half-frozen soldier walk. Then there was Joachim von Ribbentrop, Hitler's foreign minister, the high-flying "Ambassador of Might," now a wasted man seemingly devoid of emotion. Next to him sat Field Marshal Wilhelm Keitel, far livelier than the first three, and nearby sat the notorious Ernst Kaltenbrunner, chief of the Gestapo, who had reported to Heinrich Himmler. Kaltenbrunner was a younger, thirtyish man with heavy eyebrows and intense, piercing eyes. I mentioned his eyes later to one of my staff, who had had the dubious pleasure of interrogating him many months earlier. He immediately responded, "Gestapo eyes."

Admiral Dönitz was accused of several acts of aggressive warfare. The British, having nearly lost the Battle of the Atlantic and the war in 1942 through aggressive German submarine attacks, had asked to be assigned the prosecution of the case against the Germany Navy and Dönitz, and as a result, the British prosecutor was handling this case. Dönitz answered questions quickly and directly, using facts and logic to persuade the judges of his innocence, an approach not followed by most of the defendants.[2] Among other charges, he was accused of breaking the international law of submarine warfare by torpedoing British merchant ships without advance warning. Such notice would have allowed sailors to board lifeboats, enhancing their chance of survival. Combatants had often followed that gallant practice in World War I. The practice was abandoned in World War II, leading to the loss of many lives.

Dönitz was ready for this charge. The nub of his patient, detailed defense was this: Sometime during 1942, American B-24 Liberator bombers had started flying antisubmarine patrols all over the Atlantic. Before then, a submarine could surface, warn the ship, sink her, and then escape an attack from distant, hostile ships. In 1942, he said, a submarine that surfaced to warn its prey would sight an approaching American B-24 bomber on the horizon. By the time the submarine could submerge deep enough to avoid being crushed by depth charges from the B-24, it would be too late. That was why German submarines torpedoed without warning and from a submerged position.

Dönitz's attorney demonstrated an ability vastly superior to that of the counsel for the other defendants. For example, he mastered unfamiliar Anglo-Saxon legal procedures, allowing him to introduce in evidence the written testimony, called an interrogatory, of witnesses whose duties precluded their coming to the trial. He had boldly deposed Admiral Chester Nimitz, commander in chief of the United States Pacific Fleet, who admitted that submerged American submarines sank Japanese merchant vessels without warning from the first day the United States entered the war. In the end, Dönitz was found not guilty of violating the rules of submarine warfare regarding merchant ships. However, the court did subsequently find him guilty of other criminal actions and sentenced him to ten years in prison, the lightest sentence of any convicted defendant.

On the whole I was favorably impressed with the Nuremberg proceedings. I admired the clock-like precision of translations that had to cope with so many technical, military, government, and legal terms. The court maintained an atmosphere of dignity at all times. Defense lawyers and prosecutors had to stand thirty feet from the witness—there could be no psychological browbeating of witnesses. Everyone sat quietly in his place and listened placidly through phones. Even when Dönitz made typically German anti-Russian statements in the context of shooting Russian refugees, or *flüchtlinge*, in East Prussia just before the war's end, the Russian judges displayed no emotion whatsoever. German correspondents who sat near me in the visitors' gallery told me they were greatly impressed with the fairness of the trial.

Collectively, the defendants were poised, yet informal, and took a great interest in the proceedings, leaning forward in rapt attention as Dönitz and his brilliant British adversary, Sir David Maxwell-Fyfe, the deputy chief British prosecutor, exchanged niceties about whether Dönitz had been involved in ordering the murder of British naval prisoners. Maxwell-Fyfe's biting sarcasm added excitement to the trial. The American chief prosecutor, Justice Robert Jackson—on leave from the United States Supreme Court—didn't utter a word in the three days I was there, perhaps giving free rein to the British, who had a greater stake than the Americans in prosecuting Dönitz. Or maybe Jackson had been subdued by his earlier "flop" with Göring. The prosecution staff told me Jackson's inadequate preparation of the prosecution's case allowed the bold, quick-witted Göring to evade answering questions by bursting into defiant speeches justifying Nazi policies.

I tried to smoke out the opinions of Roy Steyer and his colleagues on the prosecution team as to whether all the defendants would get the death penalty. They predicted that one or two would go scot-free. Three were acquitted: Hjalmar Schacht, former president of the Reichsbank before the war, Fritz von Papen, former German minister to Austria and Turkey, and Hans Fritsche, former head of the Home Press Division of the Propaganda Ministry.[3]

The tribunal staff relished watching the twenty-three prisoners take their exercise in the courtyard at 11 AM each day. They were clearly visible through the office windows. As Hitler's lackeys trooped by, clerks would point out who was who to visitors. Security was tight for fear that fanatical German nationalists might try to liberate the prisoners. Military police were stationed all around the courthouse. The relationship between the townspeople and occupying prosecutors was formal, although trial staff, like the British in imperial India, soon developed good relationships with maids and others who helped them live in style. After hours they would repair to the only refurbished hotel for drinks, dinner, and dancing. There they went every night, unless officers gave parties in their private quarters.

Before attending Russian parties, Americans, in anticipation of excessive vodka guzzling, drank milk to line their stomachs.

Soviet intelligence had many advantages over the fledgling SSU: a long history, the Communist party's absolute power to direct or attract bright young Soviet linguists to the NKVD, and fat budgets under paranoidally security-conscious Joseph Stalin. Soviet intelligence also had no scruples about forcing people to do its bidding, even though that approach sometimes backfired. Against all Soviet advantages, we had one strong bow in our quiver: the Germans hated and dreaded the Russians, while, especially in Berlin, they liked, or at least tolerated, the Americans. Consequently, Germans periodically came forward to help the Americans spy on the Soviets, often from excellent vantage points created by the Soviets themselves. Typical was the German electrician, hired by the Soviets to wire an office, who approached us, offering to install a bug or wiretap.

Another German who came to us helped destroy an important Soviet operation. He was forced to be the driver for a Soviet-controlled German ring that kidnapped German scientists for work in the Soviet Union. Stalin, reportedly shocked when the United States exploded an atomic bomb over Hiroshima in August of 1945, immediately instructed Laventry Beria, head of the NKVD, to speed up the manufacture of that miracle weapon for the Soviet Union. Stalin wasn't actually shocked, for Soviet espionage, unknown to the West, had already penetrated the supersecret U.S. atomic laboratory at Los Alamos, New Mexico. Through a German-born British spy, Klaus Fuchs, and other lesser sources, the Soviets had obtained design data sufficient to build and explode their own atomic bomb in 1949. Of course, Stalin's top collaborators carefully shielded their penetration of atomic secrets from most people, even those in the intelligence community. Accordingly, unknowing Soviet espionage centers often undertook their own freewheeling efforts to help the Soviet Union learn how to manufacture atomic weapons. One especially dumb mission we heard about involved asking a spy to penetrate the offices of General Clay, the top American general in Berlin after Eisenhower returned to the United States, to search for possible atomic secrets. Of course, there were none there.

A more practical Soviet target included German nuclear scientists. The effort to recruit them was typically double pronged, equal parts persuasion and force. The Soviet-controlled German agents identified scientists, not just the most brilliant minds, but even high school physics teachers, as promising candidates. Soviet intermediaries would offer the more qualified among them jobs in the Crimea to do research on the atomic bomb. Some accepted. Prominent scientists who refused were slated for kidnapping. At one point the German driver of the kidnap car approached some Americans, who in turn led him to SSU. Sometimes he knew, considerably in advance, the identity of the next kidnap victim and the tactical approach by which he might be lured to a particular spot at a certain time. From him, SSU often learned which physicist was next on the kidnap list. The bigger and more important the name, the longer the advance notice, since preparations to kidnap key personnel were carefully planned. SSU, on learning of a name, would cable it to the Washington office, which would then ask people working for the Manhattan Project (the code name for the U.S. atomic project) whether the intended victim knew so much about atomic theory that, if possible, the kidnapping should be frustrated. Following the sensible British practice of protecting secrets by not exploiting them too often and thereby arousing suspicion, we "let" the spy ring kidnap perhaps three-quarters of the intended victims and arranged for only the most important physicists to avoid capture.

If my memory serves me correctly, one of those important figures was Otto Hahn, the Nobel Prize–winning German scientist who codiscovered nuclear fission and had also helped to create heavy water. During the war the British, fearing heavy water was the precursor of some nuclear fusion weapon that Germany was developing, had launched several courageous attacks on a German facility in northern Norway that manufactured heavy water. Immediately after the war, the British whisked Hahn off to England for six months to be debriefed by their scientists. He was then returned to the British zone near Hanover. Soviet intelligence understandably wanted Otto Hahn to work for Stalin on his atomic project.

Again, I'm not sure the scientist I'm thinking of was Hahn. Whatever his identity, he was a central figure in nuclear physics, and in the spring of 1946, the Soviets offered this person a well-equipped laboratory in the Crimea and U.S. $100,000 annually to conduct nuclear bomb research. When he declined, the Soviets decided to kidnap him near his residence in the British zone, not too far from the border of the Soviet zone. Shortly thereafter, they approached a close friend of their target who lived in the Soviet zone and was either a Communist or under Soviet control. Following instructions, this Soviet accomplice wrote to the scientist suggesting a picnic in the Hartz Mountains at a site near his residence. The picnic site was on a seldom-traveled road in the forest. A car with German agents would swoop into the British zone, snatch their prize, and quickly double back into Soviet territory.

Naturally, our contacts at the Manhattan Project requested that we frustrate this operation. Because the scientist resided in the British zone, I sought the cooperation of Major James Brydon, the head of MI-6's Berlin counterespionage arm, asking him to block the kidnapping in a manner that would not disclose British and American knowledge. He agreed and hit on a good strategy: have the military police stage a false documents raid, or *razzia*, over a wide area, which would coincidentally include the planned picnic site. The kidnappers would think it was sheer bad luck that they had been accidentally caught up in a document raid. The camouflage worked. Once the British had the scientist under their protection, they warned him that his friend, working for the Soviets, had set a trap and that further efforts to catch him were likely. The British suggested he go to Stockholm, beyond the reach of Soviet forces, which he did.

While my memory of the aborted kidnapping is vivid, no SSU records confirm that Hahn was the target.[4] One biography of Hahn reports that he was taken to England with other German nuclear scientists in 1945 and, after his return to Germany, was elected president of the Max Planck Society for the Advancement of Science in Berlin.[5] If the target was Hahn, did he go briefly to Stockholm, then to Berlin, and for security reasons never tell of his close shave near Hanover? On the other hand, David Murphy, later chief of the CIA station in Berlin, in 1994 found a 1946 SSU document reporting a similar Soviet-sponsored attempt to kidnap an unnamed scientist[6]; he stated in 2003 that it was common knowledge that the Soviets in 1946 were desperate to lay their hands on scientists who could help them acquire an atomic bomb and that the specific details in my account had the ring of truth.[7] Richard Helms, who at the time of the aborted kidnapping was in charge of the Eastern European desk at SSU-Washington, told me that it was "entirely plausible" that the person slated for kidnapping in this case was Hahn.[8]

The aborted kidnapping is just one example of many illustrating how the Soviets were muscle-arming their way to becoming a superpower. Significantly, the Soviet kidnapping of German nuclear scientists backfired in part. The scientists, ultimately released by the Soviets after the death of Stalin, returned to Germany where they became one of the most valuable sources of American intelligence about Soviet nuclear research."[9]

FLYING HIGH

In April 1946 I received a thrilling assignment for a twenty-nine-year-old. The top officers at the Berlin station, Dana Durand, a former Harvard associate professor who succeeded Richard Helms as chief of station, and Peter Sichel, head of SI, returned to the United States on leave and asked me to substitute for them in giving the SSU briefing to Gen. Lucius Clay's staff in the Office of Intelligence in Berlin. The Office of Intelligence was loosely related to SSU. General Clay, as the American deputy military governor, was the de facto head of military government in both the American zone and the American sector within Berlin because his technical superior in Frankfurt, the commanding general of the U.S. forces, Gen. Joseph T. McNarney, limited his actions to military matters.

The topics we discussed with the Office of Intelligence and other departments ranged from politics to espionage to military matters (we strongly advised against early release of members of the German general staff from prison camp). We also reviewed what SSU had gleaned of Soviet intentions. Our former Rhodes scholar and *Luftwaffe* pilot had reported to us that the Soviets were secretly shipping German jet planes, pilot trainers, and whole airplane factories back to the Soviet Union. Perhaps most important of all, we told Clay's staff that we were tracking Soviet efforts to frustrate democracy in their zone by developing a Communist dictatorship. Knowing that Germans hated Communists, the Soviets contrived to merge other political parties, such as the Social Democratic Party—which, before Hitler's rise, had had a considerable following in Berlin and Prussia—with the Communist Party. Two leading members of parties being forcibly merged were Jacob Kaiser and Rudolph Hermes, who also served as SI agents; they confirmed for us what the

Soviet puppet German government was actually doing (later the Communists ousted Kaiser and Hermes). General Clay's staff was keenly interested in what SSU's courageous political-penetration agents had to tell them about the puppet government.

I continued to play as hard as I worked, and by mid-June my health began to decline. I suffered stomach pains and bleeding gums, which I foolishly reported to my mother, who responded with transatlantic suggestions that I cut down on drinking and get more sleep. I wrote back that if things didn't get better, I could see the one of Hitler's physicians reputed not to be a quack. For the time being, however, I did nothing, reasoning that the symptoms were temporary and would go away.

Gradually, X-2 Berlin became confident it had learned the basics about the massive Soviet intelligence effort and how to respond to it more effectively. X-2's knowledge of Soviet intelligence had expanded exponentially ever since Allen Dulles entered Berlin with OSS on July 4, 1945. A year later, we were asked to prepare a comprehensive summary of Soviet intelligence techniques for our superiors in Washington and Heidelberg, which had replaced Wiesbaden as SSU headquarters in Germany. Presumably, they requested similar reports from all stations engaged in counterespionage work on the perimeter of the Soviet Union, such as Vienna, Stockholm, and Istanbul.

I wrote my report on ten single-spaced, legal-sized pages under my code number, AB 16, liberally assisted by an editor, AB 51. I acknowledged at the start that we had not yet unearthed top-level spy operators or gained an understanding of their techniques. The report detailed how clumsy lower-level Soviet intelligence operations were and reflected a growing confidence that the Russians were not adapting to the German culture as well as the Americans. We believed this key fact gave us one enormous advantage in our top mission of defending against Soviet intelligence.

My report reflected blissful ignorance of the fact that an operation was about to roll up a net of SI spies in the Soviet zone and send them packing to Siberia for eight years.[1] The report also failed to recognize how successful top-level Soviet intelligence had been during World War II, especially with Kim Philby and his Cambridge Five penetrating Britain's vaunted MI-6 and Klaus Fuchs and others filching the design for the American atomic bomb at Los Alamos.

In 1946, X-2 in Berlin lacked electronic surveillance of Soviet Army and diplomatic traffic. That deficiency contrasted sharply with British and

U.S. wartime access to German wireless traffic. Further, we remained woefully outmanned by Soviet intelligence and needed to concentrate our scarcer manpower on top-level thrusts by the Soviets. On March 6 Winston Churchill warned the West that "an iron curtain had descended over the [European] continent from Stettin on the Baltic to Trieste on the Adriatic," but this fact hadn't fully registered with Congress and President Truman, and so we had to make do with very little.[2]

We did know for certain, however, that Soviet intelligence sought vigorously to acquire any American secrets known to General Clay's headquarters in Berlin. How could our David fight their intelligence Goliath? One small solution formed in my mind. We should plant a skilled decoy among the secretaries working for the top members of the Office of Military Government for the United States (OMGUS). She could subtly indicate to her fellow German employees that she was susceptible to Soviet ideas, which might tempt a Soviet spy among them to seek to recruit her. This decoy would act as our double agent, penetrating the string of agents and cutouts, eventually leading to the Soviet cell, mission, and techniques.

The idea had obvious risks. It was a long-range operation that might at some point self-destruct. Americans at OMGUS might learn of the decoy's role and be indiscreet about it. Our answer was to plant the decoy without anyone's knowledge except for SSU headquarters in Heidelberg and Washington. All applicants for employment with OMGUS were checked by the CIC. We had to outwit their screening efforts and send our agent through unbeknownst to them. If she passed and should not have, it would also disclose a weakness there.

The more we reflected on the concept of Operation Decoy, the more we liked it, and our choice of bait was obvious and inevitable: Gabriel. Her sharp intelligence and talent as a multilingual secretary would cause her to swim quickly to the top on her own merits. We knew that during the war she had performed with admirable poise for Germany in delicate situations. She would be the perfect, cool double agent, and she had a strong motivation: hatred for the Russians. The only problem was her German intelligence history, which was a mile long. The straight solution, of course, was to change her name and her documentation in a way not likely to be detected by an alert CIC when it was performing its security clearance. We created new documents, establishing her place of birth and prior civilian employment in a German city far from her hometown, but where her German accent would fit and where all relevant public records had been destroyed in wartime bombing. Her code name was "Gambit."

Gabriel accepted the assignment. Maybe she had become bored with the soft life in the Joe house, typing my periodic letters on an American's impressions of Berlin, Germany, and the Soviets. Further, she liked working as an agent for me. Although at first she felt that I lacked the ruthlessness she had known in German intelligence officers, which she believed essential to success, eventually she changed her mind. Now she found my "consideration for people and ideas more likeable and effective."[3] We bonded as spymaster and agent.

Gabriel was moved from the Joe house to an unobtrusive Berlin apartment building where another tenant was a woman acquainted with an SSU officer. "I think I should warn you," Gabriel said, "that not only is she his mistress, which you probably knew, but more important she is not so loyal or discreet as he may assume. She complains to me about him often."

That show of professional alertness and loyalty impressed me.

As I started preparing Gabriel's documentation to support her job application, another attack of stomach pains and bleeding gums drove me to the army dispensary for medical help. An army doctor in Berlin, guessing it was ulcers, recommended a complete medical checkup at the American hospital in Neuilly just outside Paris, where I'd had the tight Swiss cast removed after my skiing accident. An army dentist said I had bleeding gums, a symptom of scurvy, contracted from a lack of fresh vegetables. So I flew to Paris, met up with my friend Robertine Lacquet, and took a cab to her house in Neuilly. The driver charged us three times the meter, which was considered reasonable. We had cocktails followed by a superb dinner with her parents.

The next day I went to the hospital to arrange for a complete battery of tests three days later. That gave me some time to tour. After viewing an exhibit of art looted by the Germans and restored by the Americans—paintings by Monet, Manet, van Gogh, Degas, Durer, and Rubens—Robertine and I took the train across the Île-de-France to the English Channel, passing by fields of potatoes, truck gardens, stacks of wheat being harvested, and cattle grazing placidly by meandering brooks. We stayed at Eu with a Huguenot couple who were friends of Robertine's. For dinner each of us consumed a large bowl of garlic-soaked escargot with succulent, bright red tomatoes on the side, good for my scurvy.

Like many Europeans, Robertine's friends were depressed by the devastation that war had wrought; unlike most Frenchmen, they contemplated emigrating to another country. For some reason they nominated Bolivia.

Having visited there in 1941, I quickly filled them in on the widespread poverty there, the rampant and disfiguring smallpox, and the squalid conditions I had witnessed in the high mountains at La Paz. I may have punctured their romantic illusions of escape.

Robertine and I walked to the beach below the white cliffs not far from Dieppe, where a Canadian reconnaissance raid in 1942 had been badly bloodied by alert German defenders. (This had contributed to Churchill's initial opposition to a cross-channel invasion of France.) Dieppe is halfway between Calais, where Hitler believed the Allies would land, and Caen, where they did. Strewn along the pebble beach was vivid evidence of the Germans' unsuccessful Fortress Europe. I began taking motion picture footage. Railroad rails stuck out of the water at low tide, vestiges of Erwin Rommel's Atlantic Wall designed to hold off British and American landing ships. Now sour-looking German prisoners, directed by French soldiers brandishing machine guns, were dismantling what their country had forced slave laborers to erect. Twisted steel rails, riveted together and buried in concrete, zigzagged up the beach. We walked through them, noting an occasional mine sagging from a top rail. Naked French children climbed aboard barnacled barricades where the mines had been cut off. Further out, fishermen hunted for clams and mussels.

When the haze in the distance lifted, Dieppe stood out quite clearly. The Germans prisoners, though laconic, scowled at my motion picture camera. I felt a sense of poetic justice watching these blond-haired *Blitzkriegers* painstakingly dismantling the outer rim of Fortress Europe. At high tide I swam in the surf over now-submerged steel spikes. French vacationers with sun umbrellas and picnic baskets occupied the dry part of the beach. Robertine and I lay on the pebbles and soaked up the sun.

It was a perfect time for me to advance my proposition that she come to Berlin. I offered her a job in military government as a secretary and good pay in hard currency. She would have an additional mission: date and become friendly with officers in the French Secret Service so as to determine whether the Communists had penetrated that organization. There was a danger that Communist plants might see some of the reports the Gaullists in the service had badgered SSU to give them. Robertine eagerly accepted the assignment, and I promised to complete the arrangements upon my return to Berlin.

Back in Neuilly I underwent metabolism and barium X-ray tests, and the specialists concluded that my stomach pains were caused by overwork and tension. Several days' rest in France had already helped, they said, and advised against overdoing it back in Berlin. Good luck! I paid my bill of 2,620 francs, or 30 dollars, and cabled the good news to my mother.

Upon my return to Berlin, SSU approved the assignment for Robertine, but right away it struck a snag. Military government refused to hire Robertine in the cover job we had requested. Although Robertine's Belgian parents had long ago moved to France, all three remained Belgian citizens. When we put through her application for employment, we believed her Belgian citizenship would raise no question. Many Belgians worked for the U.S. military government in Germany—nine hundred, in fact.

Inquiring as to why her application was rejected, I was told that the Belgian government had had a dispute with the U.S. military government in Germany over the military exchange rate for its Belgian employees. General Clay had got three-star-general mad and ordered all nine hundred Belgians working for the Americans back to their country. No new Belgians would be hired, not even from Paris. I'm not sure if the story was true, but it put an end to my plans for Robertine. She and I remained lifelong pen pals, and SSU never sought another agent to determine whether American intelligence could safely resume collaborating with the French Secret Service.

HOOKED ON ESPIONAGE

On returning from Paris, I finished obtaining false documents to bolster Gabriel's application to OMGUS. Soon she put in for a position as a secretary with fluent English. Lo and behold, the security clearance came, and within a few months her outstanding qualifications won her a promotion to secretary for a "cabinet" officer, that is, an official on the level immediately below General Clay. She was on her perch, just where we wanted her.

Toward the end of 1946, X-2 hit on a bold new idea for maximizing Gabriel's potential. Rather than passively waiting for her to receive a recruitment feeler from a possible unknown Soviet agent inside OMGUS, X-2 should aggressively use her to draw the attention of our top NKVD adversary, Captain Skurin. The means were at hand. Skurin had been asking his ostensible agent, double agent Hans Kemritz, for leads to German intelligence agents who might be kidnapped and converted into Soviet agents. Why not let Kemritz give Skurin Gabriel's true identity as a top German intelligence person who had the added appeal of working for one of General Clay's cabinet officers? As part of this shift in tactics, dubbed Operation Decoy, SSU wouldn't ask Kemritz to present Gabriel as a German with pro-Soviet tendencies; her war career—which, to protect her identity, I cannot reveal even now—would belie that and, being an impressive record in its own right, would attract Soviets anyway.

SSU was certain Skurin would rise to the bait, and so he did, telling Kemritz that the Soviets "had lots of information on her activities during the war" and that she "was another person . . . the Soviets had to get their hands on." The content of this interview was promptly relayed to SSU-Washington.[1] Skurin then instructed Kemritz to help lure Gabriel to the Soviet sector of Berlin. Kemritz was to cultivate her friendship and confidence in his reliability by inviting her, several times, to the theater in the American or British sectors, where she would feel safe. Later, when she was lulled into a sense of complacence, Kemritz would take her to the theater once more, this time in a Russian automobile, and as soon as she climbed in, she would be whisked off to Soviet territory.

Naturally, SSU had no intention of letting Gabriel be captured by the Soviets. Instead, they wanted to seize Skurin while he was attempting to kidnap her. X-2's ultimate objective was to persuade Skurin to work for SSU, either as a penetration agent inside the NKVD or as a defector. One can never anticipate, SSU reasoned, how an enemy agent will react in captivity. The shock of being disgraced by capture might make Skurin amenable. If not, at least his capture would quash the kidnapping operation through Kemritz. Either way, catching him red-handed trying to kidnap Gabriel would be a win-win situation for the United States.

Each side was wary. Gabriel never fell for the trap of entering an auto with Kemritz. Eventually, through Kemritz, Skurin invited Gabriel to meet him in the Soviet sector. SSU couldn't afford that risk, nor could Gabriel, and instead she invited Skurin to meet her in the American sector. He refused. By early 1947, as this cat-and-mouse game was playing out, Tom Polgar was either in charge of Operation Decoy or familiar with it. Forty-seven years later, he described what happened next:

Eventually a meeting was arranged in a remote corner of the French sector, close to the border of the Soviet sector. . . . The meeting was all set; we coordinated with the French; we had permission from the U.S. and French military governors to detain the Soviet officer [Skurin] once the meeting took place, but the Soviet just did not show. Two obvious explanations: Our plan leaked in the coordination process or the Soviets detected our elaborate surveillance and security measures. Or both, of course.[2]

After Operation Decoy ended and Gabriel's true identity had been blown to the Soviets, SSU rewarded her by obtaining a good civilian job for her in a private business firm in Berlin. Later, using her superior talent and language skills, she became a first-rate journalist in West Germany.

In July 1946 I told SSU I would stay on, without putting it in writing, then arranged for a month's leave in Washington, Westport, and New York, where I would notify my old law firm that I wouldn't be returning. In August a day train took me to Frankfurt, and from there I went by overnight sleeper to Bremerhaven. Four days later, along with three thousand troops and civilians, I boarded a Victory ship that had just returned German repatriates from Shanghai. The army gave me first-class accommodations and quickly accepted my offer to broadcast news during the nine-day voyage to New York, which, it was hoped, would relieve the troops' boredom. I boiled down U.S. Army and BBC news reports coming in on the ship's bridge and heavily larded them with my personal political opinions.

While feeding the troops eagerly awaited baseball scores—the St. Louis Cardinals were leading the Brooklyn Dodgers by one game in the National League pennant race—I also prepared them for surprises on the home front: shortages, strikes, rapid inflation (a 9 percent rise in two months), Congressional deadlock, race riots in Detroit and Harlem, and a revival of the Ku Klux Klan in the South. The broadcasts also summarized various foreign crises: Marshal Tito's Yugoslav Air Force shooting down two American planes, civil war in China, Muslim-Hindu riots in India, and the Soviet refusal to withdraw troops from northern Iran as promised. Included in the reports was this sickening fact: a defense lawyer at Nuremberg had claimed that the Gestapo had "as a whole taken no part in the mass murder of the Jews."

The crossing was anything but swift, but at least it carried no submarine threat, as had my crossing twenty-three months earlier. It seemed as if I had been away four years, not two, so much had been crammed into my long tour abroad. After docking in New York, I made a compulsory visit to SSU headquarters in Washington before hastening home to Westport. My parents met the train, and we had a joyous reunion. They were deeply thankful that I had emerged from the war unscathed, if thin. My mother was her old self, vivacious and inclined to show me off to her friends. It was touching, not to mention embarrassing, when, at a large tea given to promote local artists, a stream of portly ladies came up to me to bill and coo over my "wonderful accomplishments overseas."[3]

In September I went down to 2 Wall Street to see William Donovan at the law firm. In his civilian clothes he appeared as if he had never left the premises. In fact, he had left military service only eight or nine months earlier, after President Truman had rejected his recommendation that the United States create a permanent foreign intelligence service and abruptly terminated OSS. General Donovan had been unceremoniously reassigned to duty with the assistant secretary of war.[4] From there, he had served briefly as deputy to Justice Jackson, the chief American prosecutor at the Nuremberg trial. Donovan had suggested that the Nuremberg prosecutors should conduct their cases in a manner most likely to convince the German public of their war guilt by exposing Nazi falsehoods and crimes. Justice Jackson spurned this advice, preferring to make straightforward, objective presentations for historians.[5] In 1946 Donovan returned to his law firm as chief rainmaker, heavily in need of money.[6]

Walter Berry, his secretary, ushered me into the large corner office overlooking Wall Street. Donovan's cherubic Irish face, blue eyes, and careful dress instantly impressed me. He wasn't tall, yet his magnetic personality radiated warmth as he rose from his large desk and crossed the room to shake my hand. Addressing me by my first name as if we were old friends, he asked about Berlin and the service. I began bubbling over with stories of the hair-raising challenges of intelligence, whereupon he abruptly cut in. "The United States," he said, sensing that I didn't plan to return to his firm, "is still an isolationist nation. If you go into the intelligence service, you'll want to be an ambassador at fifty, a position where you can make policy." This was in the era before instant telecommunications allowed all crucial decisions to be made at the top in Washington, thereby greatly reducing the role of ambassadors in foreign policy.

"But where will foreign service get you in ten years?" he went on bluntly. "It's not certain. This country has not yet come to choosing even its minor leaders from the ranks of the foreign service. If you want to make something of yourself at fifty, go back to Hartford, Connecticut, establish yourself in the law, and be active in the Republican Party. That's how to get appointed ambassador."

His strong advice, which caught me by surprise, was both disturbing and plausible. It had seemed that an upward path in intelligence would depend on merit rather than campaign contributions. I weighed Donovan's sobering advice for several days, then reluctantly decided he was right.

In late September I traveled to Washington and found that two good friends in Germany, Sid and Wilma Taber Lennington, were home on leave. They wanted me to stay in the intelligence service and when I told them I probably wouldn't, we had a sad farewell. If they felt that Donovan's advice was partly motivated by a desire to have me back in his firm (I'm sure it wasn't), they were too polite to express their opinion. During my time there I called on Richard Helms to tender my resignation, then confirmed it in a bland, three-sentence letter on October 1, 1946. The next day, I wrote Tom Polgar asking him to ship home all my possessions remaining in Berlin. I felt very sad to be leaving exciting espionage work against what I felt was a major threat to the United States, but I knew that Donovan was probably right in suggesting that law, in the long run, offered me a better career.

Now I needed a job. I could ask the firm to take me back, but remembered its standing advice to aspiring young lawyers: acquire early one or two years of intensive trial experience, so that you could better advise clients of the risks, rewards, and expenses of potential litigation. Now seemed the ideal time to get that experience. I became a staff attorney at the criminal branch of the Legal Aid Society at 100 Centre Street in Manhattan, the building familiarly known as the Tombs, thinking I might return to the firm in eighteen months. My pay was less than one-half what I had earned in Berlin and lacked its large perks, but the work was exciting. Legal Aid defended those too poor to hire a lawyer. The cases were straight out of Dickens with a modern twist—Harlem gang fights, robbery, assault, breaking and entering, burglary, forgery, shoplifting, just about everything but murder and arson.

Although I took my thirteen months of trial work seriously, I couldn't keep espionage out of my mind and corresponded frequently with former colleagues and spies, including Karl Johann Wiberg, Zig-Zag, Gabriel, and Barbara Güttler. The winter of 1946 to 1947 was Berlin's coldest in a hundred years, and in December Barbara wrote in desperation,

[T]he people have just enough to eat not to starve. Most of the families which sold their porcelain, carpets, and furniture to get money to buy fat and meat on the black market . . . have nothing more to sell and are no longer able to buy black-food [sic]. People have no . . . coal to heat rooms. . . . Old people are dying like flies. . . . There is no water in the houses because all is frozen. My kitchen is a large ice-box and the bathroom, too. My feet are ice-blocks. I have to get to bed quickly for there it is a little warmer.[7]

This letter was followed by a plea in February:

My ideal is to go to the U.S. . . . They always say here that there is only the possibility when you marry an American—what concerns me is I never had a friend among GI's except you. . . . I believe you enjoyed our friendship as much as I did. . . . I should like to write to you permanently once a week—say Sunday—and for you to do the same thing.
Listen, Puttiput, isn't it possible for me to get a job over there in N.Y.

(for instance, I could write a lot for you)?????. . . Think about it, I do really think we could work perfectly together.[8]

Gabriel's letters bemoaned the bread freezing solid as stone and her apartment where the temperature was minus six degrees Celsius. She was rescued from the cold when Zig-Zag gave her his lined, air force sleeping bag, for which he had no need in the heated Joe house. On one cold February night, she wrote, sixty Berliners froze to death. The Russians were deporting able-bodied men on two hours' notice to work in the Soviet Union. Her brother had gone into hiding to avoid such deportation. Berliners hissed the opening of Chekhov's *Cherry Orchard*, shouting, "We have enough of the Russians; we don't want to see them on the stage, too."[9]

My old colleague Dana Durand sympathized with German sufferings during the winter: "The Krauts have certainly done penance enough for all the collective sins of the Nazis, and memories of this ordeal should be enough to chasten a whole generation."[10] The flow of letters from Germany reflecting such suffering and desperation did little to dispel my thoughts of Europe and, in fact, drove me to write articles on the politics of Germany, the Russian threat, and the need for a wiser American foreign policy. I submitted them to the *Atlantic Monthly, Foreign Affairs, The Yale Review*, and *Mercury* to no avail, then even finished two hundred pages of an espionage novel set in Berlin, which I abandoned when a friend told me it was no good.

Late in 1946, an SSU officer from Washington phoned me to meet him at an obscure hotel on Seventh Avenue in Manhattan. He invited me to rejoin the SSU as chief of mission in Stockholm. SSU was consolidating operations in four Scandinavian countries under the Stockholm head. My special assignment would be to dispatch American spies by boat across the Baltic into the Soviet Union. That, he said, was one of the most effective of very few ways to obtain badly needed intelligence from within the tightly sealed Soviet Union. The assignment was extremely dangerous. He said SSU-Washington admired my work in Berlin and that the X-2 experience there would be invaluable in the effort to penetrate the Soviet Union. Intrigued, I mulled this over with the obsession of a twenty-year-old thinking about sex. I was hooked on espionage, and the withdrawal symptoms were severe.

But there was a lot more at stake. I was almost thirty and unmarried, and while Swedish women struck me as good prospects, there was a big hitch. Regulations forbade a secret service operative from marrying a foreign national other than a British subject without a bureaucratic security clearance. In the end, I concluded that returning to espionage in Europe, even with a promotion, wouldn't be worth the risk of not finding a good wife there. Moreover, Major General Donovan's advice against an espionage career was reverberating in my mind. It was a fortunate decision, for as it happened, the cross-Baltic espionage effort turned out to be a "total failure."[11] The Soviets captured and shot every last agent. Furthermore, the offered four-country position never came into being; Stockholm remained in charge of only Stockholm—no Oslo, no Helsinki, no Copenhagen added luster to the assignment.

As I've mentioned, several of the intelligence agents with whom I worked in Berlin eventually came to a sad end—Karl Johann Wiberg, Heinz Krull (Zig-Zag), and Hans Kemritz. That wasn't the case with all my colleagues, however. Robertine Lacquet, ever one to land on her feet in any situation, having been in Berlin in 1943 and Paris in 1945, moved to New York in 1947. She became the private secretary to Mrs. Ogden Reid, publisher of the *New York Herald Tribune* from 1948 to 1950.[12] Robertine entertained me aboard the *Normandie* (formerly the German *Europa*), the prize of the French Line, on her maiden voyage after her rehabilitation following the war. The *Normandie* subsequently burned and capsized in New York Harbor. Later Robertine returned to France, married an orthopedic surgeon, and often rode to the hounds on weekends in England.

Norman Holmes Pearson went back to Yale as an admired English professor. Taking seriously our oath not to reveal British espionage secrets, he never talked to students about what he had done in London. However, he did persuade J. C. Masterman of MI-5, with whom he had worked closely in London, to commission the Yale University Press to publish his definitive *The Double-Cross System in the War of 1939 to 1945*. Pearson wrote the sixteen-page preface.

The SSU officers whom I most admired in Berlin went on to prominent careers in the CIA. Allen Dulles became its director long before the ill-fated Bay of Pigs invasion of Castro's Cuba in 1961 caused President Kennedy to ask for his resignation. Somewhat later, Richard Helms became director of the CIA, and his vast knowledge, objectivity, and level-headed leadership made him the finest of CIA directors. Eventually, President Nixon exiled Helms to Iran where he served as ambassador to the shah. Nixon, ever paranoid, wanted to get Helms out of Washington because he couldn't abide the CIA chief's professional objectivity. Helms had refused Nixon's request that the CIA assist in covering up Watergate.

Peter Sichel, the brilliant and affable head of SI in Berlin, became chief of the CIA's Berlin station after the Soviet blockade in 1948 and ultimately rose to head the CIA mission in Hong Kong in 1959. At that time his family's business—Sichel and Sons, importers and wine merchants in New York—lacked an heir to run it, so he left the CIA to assume that responsibility.

Tom Polgar became chief of station in Mexico, Saigon, Germany, and elsewhere. He briefed George H. W. Bush when Bush served briefly as head of the CIA and worked closely with Henry Kissinger on Vietnam affairs from 1972 to 1975. Polgar learned from Kissinger when he visited Vietnam that President Nixon planned to dismiss Richard Helms as head of the CIA. Polgar then forewarned Helms.[13] Polgar later served as a policy analyst for the U.S. Senate Select Committee investigating the Iran-Contra scandal during President Reagan's administration.

Elizabeth Fitzgerald, whom I met in Berlin and again in Nuremberg, moved to New York City in 1946 and took a job as a writer with the advertising department of the Metropolitan Life Insurance Company. Roy Steyer, through whom I met her, returned from Nuremberg to New York where he resumed his career as an outstanding trial lawyer at Sullivan and Cromwell. In 1946 and 1947 Elizabeth, Roy, and I attended various parties for OSS and Nuremberg veterans. In October 1947 Elizabeth and I were married in Milwaukee, her hometown, to which we moved in 1949 from New York where I joined an enterprising new law firm, later transferring to what became Wisconsin's second largest law firm. It offered me interesting cases, including a high-stakes Lake Michigan water pollution suit in the U.S. Supreme Court and many controversial political-legal fights—sometimes as a member of a Wisconsin state or regional advisory commission—over land-use, environment, freeway routes, municipal boundaries, and urban sprawl, all becoming the heart of my book, *Greater Milwaukee's Growing Pains, 1950–2000: An Insider's View.*

Over the years since leaving foreign intelligence, I have often reflected on its published ups and downs. I was shocked but not completely surprised by the total failure of the CIA (and FBI) to detect in advance terrorist plans for the September 11 attack on the Twin Towers and the Pentagon. How could the United States, I wondered, have been blindsided again as it was at Pearl Harbor, the very event that directly led to the creation of OSS and, later, the CIA? The answer is far from simple.

Sadly, I believe, the CIA's effectiveness had started to decline decades earlier. During its golden era between 1947 and the early 1970s, the CIA succeeded in penetrating many of the enemy's inner secrets through moles inside Soviet intelligence. One that comes to mind is Oleg Penkovsky, whose information supporting the opinion that Khrushchev was bluffing during the Cuban missile crisis helped prevent the Cold War from turning nuclear. The CIA's achievements in those days, in my mind, can be attributed primarily to three phenomena: risk-taking, top-flight personnel; perceptive, informed and unbiased analysis; and government oversight that supported foreign intelligence while carefully protecting its need for objective professionalism.

Those vital phenomena had started to weaken by the 1970s, if not earlier. The legislative and executive branches took turns bashing the CIA. In 1975 Senator Frank Church and Congressman Otis Pike leaked many classified documents to the press, one of which included the names and addresses of certain undercover CIA officers abroad, thereby risking their lives and setting back the recruitment of good case officers and new agents. Through fear of being pilloried for publicized failures, the CIA gradually morphed into a bureaucracy that was risk averse.

Moreover, as this book relates, President Nixon tried to force CIA director Richard Helms to keep the FBI from investigating the Watergate burglary by falsely stating, in effect, "Hands off. What's going on there is a CIA operation." Helms refused, and Nixon sent him into a virtual exile in Teheran that chilled the CIA and sent a bad message to Congress. It's inconceivable that a British prime minister would request an MI-6 head to block an investigation of a burglary he had commissioned. James Schlesinger came in as Nixon's CIA director for months with the self-stated mission of breaking up the "gentleman's club," Nixon's goal being to "get rid of the clowns—cut personnel 40 percent." Schlesinger fired or forced to resign over one thousand employees,[14] including many senior officers, particularly former OSS types, even though many were performing well. Jimmy Carter's CIA director, Stansfield Turner, continued the practice. The purges wrecked morale.

Perhaps the most fundamental reason for the CIA's decline was a gradual loss of ability to attract and keep imaginative, risk-taking linguists, persons of the caliber of those who once ran penetration agents in Moscow or planned the tunnel under the Berlin Wall that enabled technicians to tap all Soviet cable traffic between Berlin and Moscow. Bright graduates of the finest universities joined the CIA in droves early in the Cold War, but their numbers dropped after the draft ended in 1973. They declined further in the mid-1980s as the end of the Cold War approached, the booming private sector siphoned off more and more talent, and colleges stopped permitting the CIA to recruit on campus. Increasingly, prized experts on foreign lands found service in third-world countries unappealing, especially if they were married to a gifted, working spouse who could scarcely find a good job in key third-world cities like Istanbul, Cairo, Baghdad, and Teheran. It didn't help matters that security clearances were protracted, lasting sometimes for a year. Rather than waiting, good prospects often moved on to greener pastures.

Meanwhile, political correctness began favoring diversity over merit. Mediocre officers were no longer weeded out. The most infamous example is Aldrich Ames, whose lavish lifestyle should have clued CIA higher-ups into his treasonous activity. Tragically, Ames's high living went unnoticed, and in the 1980s the information he fed to the Soviets, along with that of the FBI's Robert Hanssen, led to the execution or imprisonment of all CIA agents in Moscow.

By that time, the CIA was so weakened by bureaucratic inertia that it failed—despite numerous terrorist attacks on U.S. installations overseas and the bombing of the Twin Towers in 1993—to shift missions from a Soviet-centered Cold War stance to a stance centered on terrorism originating in the Middle East. By September 11 there were scant few in the CIA who spoke Arabic and almost none who spoke any of the many languages of Afghanistan, a safe haven for Al Qaeda terrorist training camps. Had the CIA had more Arab, Pashto, or Parsi speakers, it might have—if blessed by bold leadership—successfully trolled for an almost inconceivable defector among the Al Qaeda fanatics or worked more effectively with the tough, capable intelligence organizations in Egypt, Jordan, and Pakistan, whose own self-interest would have impelled them to give priority to unmasking antiregime Al Qaeda terrorist cells.

In the wake of September 11, Washington's various responses to the CIA seem likely both to strengthen and weaken its intelligence capabilities. Agreement in 2002 between President Bush and Congress led to the appointment of the bipartisan Kean or 9/11 Commission to discover the root causes of America's weakened intelligence capabilities, which could lead to needed reforms, but probably won't because history has demonstrated that the public and politicians have neither the patience nor the sophistication to adopt and adhere to the requisite measures. The government also sharply increased the CIA budget, which will help in the recruitment of badly needed people fluent in Arabic and other Middle Eastern languages. By May 2003 the Senate Select Committee on Intelligence unanimously recommended the creation of a program to encourage college students to pursue intelligence careers, which would be the intelligence community's equivalent of the military's ROTC. The committee also suggested that intelligence agencies be allowed to hire linguists and other specialists on short notice, presumably by speeding up the cumbersomely designed, lackadaisically pursued security-clearance process. In fact, the process had already sped up. By mid 2003 applications to join the CIA had trebled from 2000, and three-quarters of the latest recruits were proficient in foreign languages. However, the CIA director of human resources told the press that if they walked into the room, he could hire "100 more native Arabic speakers if otherwise qualified. Same with Chinese. Same with Persian. Same with Urdu."

The CIA's paramilitary arm performed brilliantly after September 11. Its special forces behind enemy lines, proud descendants of OSS's World War II guerrilla fighters in France, Burma, and the Balkans, were the first to engage in Afghanistan and made critical contributions to the decisive precision bombing of Taliban and Al Qaeda forces. Later, a CIA armed, pilotless predator tracked and killed an Al Qaeda leader crossing the Yemen desert.

The CIA's impressive paramilitary feats in Afghanistan and, in particular, the ongoing steps to strengthen the CIA are offset by how the Bush administration handled, or mishandled, intelligence before the war in Iraq. Secretary of Defense Donald Rumsfeld and his influential deputy, Paul Wolfowitz, convinced, or at least wishing to prove, that Iraq had ties with Al Qaeda, as well as large stockpiles of weapons of mass destruction, became annoyed at the CIA's inability to verify their beliefs. To search for evidence supporting their case, they then created a small unit at the Defense Department, blandly labeled Special Plans.

Special Plans sought Iraqi defectors as sources and invited the help of Ahmad Chalabi's Iraqi National Congress (INC), a group of Iraqi émigrés. The INC was motivated to give the Defense Department what it wanted to hear in order to win Pentagon support for its own agenda, which was to obtain a role in the future initial government of Iraq, which Chalabi did obtain, but later lost. Special Plans unwisely delegated the interrogation of defectors and even the reporting of what they said, not to the CIA, but to the INC, which was untrained in intelligence. Not surprisingly, the INC reported dramatic incidents to Special Plans and leaked some of them to the press. One account said the defector had trained with Al Qaeda at a camp where they received instruction on chemical and biological weapons, but later interviews by the CIA using its own interpreter revealed the defector to have said only that the camp was for *fedayeen* and that there were no Al Qaeda and no biological or chemical weapons. According to one defector, the September 11 attack was carried out by people trained by Iraq. Another defector claimed that Iraqis had taught certain Arabs how to highjack a Boeing 707, but later both a former CIA officer and a former military analyst stated that the training was for counterterrorism—specifically how to abort the highjacking of a 707, there having been a number of plane highjackings in Iraq. Still another defector described seeing a facility for making chemical and biological weapons hidden underneath a Baghdad hospital, but UN inspectors who went to the site found no supporting evidence.

The truthfulness of these and other "intelligence" reports from defectors, some of which were leaked to the press to justify the invasion of Iraq, has been called into question. More importantly, no weapons of mass destruction have yet been found in Iraq.

Even more damaging to America's reputation for accuracy was the persistent habit of forceful neoconservatives in various agencies—defense, state, and the vice president's office—to insist on receiving raw intelligence without the benefit of vetting, that is, double-checking for veracity, by intelligence professionals, and to interpret it to support their preconceived conclusions.[15] This bypassing of the intelligence vetting process allowed false reports to appear in various speeches by the president and vice president, leading up to the invasion of Iraq in March 2003. Two excerpts from the president's State of the Union Address on January 28, 2003, illustrate their rash nature. Bush said, "Iraq had up to 30,000 warheads, 500 tons of chemical weapons, and 25,000 liters of anthrax . . . and a secret push for atomic weapons,"[16] and uttered these notorious sixteen weasel words: "The British government has learned that Saddam Hussein recently sought significant quantities of uranium from Africa"[17]— notwithstanding earlier CIA advice that reports of Iraqi efforts to obtain uranium from Nigeria were dubious (the CIA later concluded they were based on forged documents.)

Unfortunately, the United States, faced with overwhelming international skepticism about its stated objectives in going to war with Iraq, had staked—perhaps unwittingly—its international reputation on the reliability of its intelligence concerning prewar Iraqi capabilities and activities. One thing is certain: the Bush administration's persistent bypassing of the CIA to develop intelligence fitting its agenda damaged the United States' reputation and gravely demoralized and weakened the CIA.

The CIA's sharp decline in recent decades will be difficult to reverse. My own limited experience with intelligence during and immediately after World War II and my observations of CIA successes and failures in the years since then have convinced me that the United States needs a foreign intelligence agency that is strong and objective, not politicized. If we fail to rejuvenate and respect our intelligence system, we risk being blindsided yet again.

Source Notes

Introduction

1. Russian soldiers told American medics that during the war Russian troops infected with venereal disease were sent immediately to the front lines.

2. *Kommandatura* was the Russian name for the four-power Allied Control Council in which the occupation forces attempted, mostly in vain, to agree on common policies to be enforced in their respective occupation zones in Germany.

Chapter 1

1. In *Roosevelt's Secret War* (p. 439), Joseph Persico writes that 334 B-29 bombers killed between 80,000 and 100,000 Japanese on the night of March 9–10, 1945.

2. Keegan, *Times Atlas,* 196.

Chapter 2

1. Brown, *Last Hero,* 165.

2. Waller, *Unseen War in Europe,* 217.

3. However, Roosevelt did not give Donovan the authority to commission civilian recruits in any military rank he chose. Roosevelt gave that power to Alfred McCormack, chief of the War Department's Special Branch, which handled the sensitive distribution of the Allies' greatest war secret, the deciphered German and Japanese military messages.

4. Brown, *Last Hero,* 173.

5. Brown, *Last Hero,* 301.

6. Waller, *Unseen War in Europe,* 217.

Chapter 3

1. Historians generally agree that British code breaking was the top intelligence feat of the war, perhaps equaled only by the Americans' breaking the Japanese naval code (Magic), which enabled them to surprise and crush the Japanese fleet at Midway in 1942. General Eisenhower said that breaking German codes was the equivalent of his being given a tank army with two years' experience, of which he had none.

2. Naftali, 208.

3. Naftali, 203.

4. Ed Washburn, a classmate of the author's at the Army Air Corps Intelligence School in Harrisburg, Pennsylvania, was recruited from there for Special Branch, the agency that analyzed and distributed the top-secret Japanese and German intercepted messages to a most limited audience. In 1994, he sent the author his memorandum describing Special Branch's operations, written for his fiftieth reunion at Yale, including the only printed statement ever read by the author saying that the Japanese did learn, through the Yamamoto shooting, that the U.S. Navy had broken their code. The Japanese then changed their code and the Navy broke the new one in three weeks. Compare Joseph Persico, *Roosevelt's Secret War*, p.190, in which he states that the Japanese never learned that their code had been broken.

5. Naftali, *X-2*, 214.

6. Masterman, *The Double-Cross System*, xiv.

7. MI-5 (domestic intelligence) said to OSS personnel that they had "doubled" or neutralized all such agents. Naftali's stupendous research of records disclosed that by February 1944 MI-5 controlled "more than twenty" double agents of the *Abwehr* and that the *Abwehr* had not attempted to send another agent into England after late 1942, being satisfied with its coverage from existing agents, *all* of whom had been doubled by MI-5. Naftali, *X-2*, 511.

8. Winks, *Cloak and Gown*, 281.

9. The key double agents were named "Tate" and "Garbo." Naftali, *X-2*, 650.

10. Hesketh, *Fortitude*, 202, 208.

11. Winks, *Cloak and Gown*, 300.

12. Naftali, *X-2*, 650.

Chapter 4

1. Letter, Owen Keeling to Amelia Cutler, January 4, 1945.

2. A March 15, 1945, recommendation for the promotion of 2d Lt. Richard W. Cutler to first lieutenant by Maj. Thomas E. Lee recited that both the B-29 Bomb Group and the MEDTO OSS desk in Washington had earlier started his promotion process only to drop it when he was transferred out.

3. Winks, *Cloak and Gown,* 287

4. Winks, *Cloak and Gown,* 288

5. The change of assignment took effect November 1 and authorized the author to attend the British SHAEF school on counterintelligence in occupied territories.

6. Winks, *Cloak and Gown,* 300.

7. Keegan, *Second World War,* 442.

8. Two of the 106th Division's three regiments surrendered, but the 28th Infantry fought tenaciously for three days against five attacking Panzer divisions before its middle regiment was overrun. Letter to the author, July 3, 1995, from John D. Dahlberg of Milwaukee, who was a lieutenant in the battle.

9. Oral report to the author, December 1994, by one of those veterans, Lt. Thomas B. Fifield, then of Janesville, Wisconsin, but later of Milwaukee.

10. Letter to the author from Lawrence de Neufville, January 3, 1995.

11. Keegan, *Second World War,* 445

Chapter 5

1. The British public named the 1940 to 1941 bombing of London and fifteen other cities the Blitz after the German war against Poland, which the Germans called *Blitzkrieg,* or Lightning War (Keegan, *Times Atlas of the Second World War,* 53).

2. For a more gruesome statistical and judgmental description of the bombing damage, see Stiegler, *London at War,* 118–28, 158, 160–1, 179–81, 267–74. He concludes that a third of the city was all but destroyed. The author disagrees, unless one includes every building suffering minor damage as being destroyed. In any event, the utter destruction in the center of Berlin—for dozens of contiguous blocks—was much greater.

3. In the Battle of Britain the RAF defeated the *Luftwaffe* by exciting dogfights between Spitfires and Messerschmitt 109s mostly between the English Channel and London. Between July and October 1940 the Germans lost 1,733 planes to the RAF's 915. On September 15, 1940, the RAF shot down sixty, or 30 percent, of the two hundred German bombers attacking London. Hitler then called off the invasion. The defeat of the *Luftwaffe* in 1940 saved Britain from an invasion that her badly depleted Army could scarcely have repelled. Some 2,500 young pilots had been responsible for preserving England from invasion, leading to Churchill's second immortal gem: "Seldom have so many owed so much to so few" (Keegan, *Times Atlas,* 52, 101–2; *Second World War,* 101).

4. Stiegler, *London at War,* 267, 272.

5. Winks, *Cloak and Gown,* 300.

6. Stiegler, *London at War,* 298.

7. Churchill Club's four-page brochure, 1944.

Chapter 6

1. Casey, *Secret War against Hitler,* 185.
2. Persico, *Piercing the Reich,* 12.
3. Casey, *Secret War against Hitler,* 185. In a conference during the Battle of the Bulge with the heads of British Secret Intelligence Service (SIS) and Special Operations Executive (SOE) (sabotage), Casey found them very skeptical about the ability of OSS to station and sustain agents inside Germany.
4. Persico, *Piercing the Reich,* 195.
5. Persico, *Piercing the Reich,* 161; Casey, *Secret War against Hitler,* 162.
6. Persico, *Piercing the Reich,* 333; Warner, *Office of Strategic Services,* 22; Casey, *Secret War against Hitler,* 198. Casey reports that OSS-London dropped eighty-eight two-man teams into Germany, but seven were apparently French. He omits agents parachuted from Italy and those sent over ground from Switzerland and Sweden.
7. Persico, *Piercing the Reich,* 114. However, Peter Sichel, one of Henry Hyde's team, reported in 2002 that he sent thirty agents into Germany, but only three, or 10 percent, were killed by the mines. E-mail of Peter Sichel to author, December 2002.
8. Persico, *Piercing the Reich,* 258.
9. Persico, *Piercing the Reich,* 333.
10. SI Operations Report, April 7, 1945, National Archives, Record Group 226, Entry 99.
11. Keegan, *Second World War,* 497.
12. James Murphy, chief of X-2 Washington, campaigned at least from October 1943 to learn the names of SI agents and check them for security against ISOS. In 1944 when the U.S. military in Italy objected to SI's carelessly hiring a German agent, Donovan finally overruled SI (Naftali, *X-2,* 391–92, 591). X-2 vetting of SI agents then started.
13. Winks, *Cloak and Gown,* 532.
14. Recommendation for promotion of 2d Lt. Richard W. Cutler to Promotion Board, OSS, by Maj. Hans V. Tofte, March 15, 1945.

Chapter 8

1. Letter from Tom Polgar to the author, August 22, 1994.
2. Letter from Timothy Naftali to the author, July 23, 1989. Naftali assisted Professor Robin Winks with research for *Cloak and Gown.* Later, he reviewed all declassified OSS and SSU documents relating to X-2 operations in London and Berlin while preparing his Harvard Ph.D. thesis on the origins of American counterespionage. During that work, he interviewed the author and prepared

summaries of what OSS and SSU records said about the author's assignments and performance within X-2.

3. Letter from Lt. Col. I. I. Milne to Norman H. Pearson, June 6, 1945.

4. Certificate of Merit for Richard W. Cutler, signed by Col. James R. Forgan, June 30, 1945.

Chapter 9

1. "Werewolf" is the mythologically romantic name for "guerrilla." Hitler's propaganda chief, Josef Goebbels, successfully peddled the falsehood that the Nazis would harass future Allied occupation troops from an Alpine redoubt. On March 28, 1945, Eisenhower, believing in the redoubt notion, diverted troops southward from their thrust toward Berlin (Waller, *Unseen War in Europe*, 371–72).

2. This was the greatest tank battle of World War II in August of 1943. More than nine thousand tanks on both sides slugged it out. The Soviets decisively beat the Germans, who thereafter were always on the defensive. The West heard little of this massive German defeat, but the Germans knew.

3. Grose, *Gentleman Spy*, 214.

4. Naftali, *X-2*, 417.

5. Persico, *Roosevelt's Secret War*, 251.

6. Naftali, *X-2*, 419, 424, 429.

7. Waller, *Unseen War in Europe*, 302–3.

8. Petersen, *From Hitler's Door*, 263, 265.

9. Edwin J. Putzell Jr., assistant to General Donovan at OSS, in remarks at a symposium at the sixtieth anniversary of the founding of OSS, held at the CIA, in Langley, Virginia, on June 7, 2002. There are numerous accounts of unrecorded FDR–Donovan conversations. Many did not happen, but this one probably did because Putzell was an aide highly trusted by Donovan—he personally carried Donovan's messages to Roosevelt.

10. However, in the 1980s and 1990s the United States neglected human intelligence in favor of code breaking, spy satellites, and technological intelligence. Perhaps reflecting or contributing to that shift, in 1989 British historian John Keegan erroneously underestimated the value in World War II of human intelligence ("Humint"). He said it was no more than "marginal" or "patchy" when compared with "the substantial contribution of code breaking (signals intelligence, or 'Sigint') to the World War II strategy" (Keegan, *Second World War*, 497).

Keegan was writing before John Waller, in *The Unseen War in Europe*, documented many epic achievements of espionage. They included Britain's Double Cross, which deceived the Germans as to the landings in North Africa and Normandy, Dulles's fruitful contact with both Fritz Kolbe in Berlin and the German opposition to Hitler, and the Soviet spy Richard Sorge's efforts in Tokyo, which saved Moscow from the Germans. Sorge advised Stalin in 1941 that Japan was about to start a Pacific war to the south. Stalin secretly moved troops from east Siberia in the nick of time to relieve Moscow from the German Army at its gates. There were two other highly touted spies: Lucy in Switzerland, who relayed German military plans to the Soviets before they decisively defeated the Germans at Kursk in 1943, and most notorious of all, Kim Philby, the Soviet mole inside MI-6 who passed the western Allies' secrets to Stalin throughout the war and for many years afterward.

11. These figures appear in OSS records declassified by the CIA and were reviewed and relayed to the author in a letter from Tim Naftali, July 23, 1989.

12. The author believed Allen Dulles to have been chief of mission then, but OSS records say that Colonel Suhling was. Dulles was head for Germany and was transferred at some point to Berlin, perhaps being replaced as chief of the Wiesbaden station by Suhling.

13. Letter to the author from Tim Naftali, July 23, 1989.

14. Waller, *Unseen War in Europe,* 365.

Chapter 10

1. Author's letter to "Folks Back Home," *Westport Town Crier,* August 20, 1945.

2. Address by Stephen E. Ambrose, director of the Eisenhower Center at the University of New Orleans, to the Rotary Club in Milwaukee, May 16, 1995. Eisenhower's statement probably also appears in Ambrose's *Eisenhower: Soldier and President,* 1990.

3. Author's letter to "Folks Back Home."

4. Letter to the author from J. Edward Lumbard Jr., September 10, 1945.

5. Troy, *Donovan and the CIA,* 226–229, 256, 258, 281–2, and 287–304.

Chapter 11

1. Beevor, *Fall of Berlin,* 429.

2. In fact, Stalin's secret police had on May 5 dug up Hitler's burned body from its grave near the *Reichskanzlei,* carted his skull to Moscow, and concealed the fact from the world and even Marshall Zhukov, Berlin's conqueror, for twenty years. "Stalin's strategy, quite apparently, was to associate the West with Nazism by pretending that the British or Americans must be hiding him. Rumours already circulated . . . that he had escaped through tunnels or by aeroplane . . . at the last moment, and was hiding in American-occupied Bavaria" (Beevor, *Fall of Berlin,* 399).

3. Grose, *Gentleman Spy*, 78.

4. The Office of War Information, the wartime propaganda arm of the U.S. government.

Chapter 12

1. Tempelhof was Berlin's airport, which the author had studied eighteen months earlier at the Army Air Force Intelligence School at Harrisburg, Pennsylvania. There, aerial photos "showed the field jammed with ME 109s and FW 190s used for the defense of Berlin. After the war, there were a dozen C-47s, two or three Mitchells, a Flying Fortress, and the usual assortment of cubs and other liaison planes" (letter from the author to his family, September 24, 1945).

2. Berlin's prewar population of 4.5 million had dropped to 3 million by the end of the war, but still vastly exceeded that of Munich, Leipzig, Hamburg, Düsseldorf, or Frankfurt.

3. Berlin lay 118 miles north of Czechoslovakia, 100 miles south of the Baltic Sea, due south of Stockholm, and 52 miles west of the new postwar border of Poland on the Oder River. It also lay 110 miles east of the British zone of occupation, this being the border that was to become the Iron Curtain dividing Western Europe from the postwar Soviet empire to the east.

4. Ryan, *The Last Battle*, 520.

5. The Soviet sector contained the city's center, the *Reichskanzlei*, the kaiser's palace, and the principal government buildings. The American sector included the western reaches, many parks and lakes, plus Schoeneberg, later to become the capital of West Berlin and the site in 1961 where President John F. Kennedy reassured Berliners with his enthusiastically received greeting, *Ich bin ein Berliner*. The remark was intended to show American support for the Berliners after the Russians permitted the German Communist puppet state to erect the notorious Berlin Wall in 1961, which cut off East from West Berlin and East Germany from West Germany until it was dismantled in 1989. The British sector encompassed the Tiergarten, the *Reichstag*, and the principal shopping street, the Kurfurstendamm.

6. Author's official report of December 20, 1945, to Norman Pearson in Washington as described by Timothy Naftali after reviewing OSS–SSU files, in a letter to the author, July 23, 1993.

7. Author's letter to friends, "Random Contacts with the Russians in Berlin," November 26, 1945, 4.

Chapter 13

1. Germany developed a jet airplane fighter long before the United States did. Eisenhower reportedly said that if Germany had developed the jet fighter a year earlier, the war in Europe might have been a draw.

2. October 10, 1945, report of Crosby Lewis, then chief of X-2 Germany, found in CIA files; letter to the author from David Murphy, former CIA officer in Berlin in the 1950s, November 9, 1993.

3. In *The Last Battle* (p. 138) Ryan attributes a role to Wiberg even larger than the role Joseph Persico presents in *Piercing the Reich* (p. 317).

4. Ryan, *The Last Battle*, 401.

5. Letter to the author from Frau Karl Johann Wiberg, 1988.

6. Radio address by Churchill, October 1, 1939; Bartlett's *Familiar Quotations*, 14th ed. (Boston: Little Brown, 1968), 920.

7. Letter from Tom Polgar to the author, October 31, 1995.

8. Report to Washington by Crosby Lewis, chief of X-2 Germany, October 10, 1945, as quoted in a letter to the author from David E. Murphy, November 9, 1993. Murphy was then writing the history of American-Soviet counterespionage in Berlin during the Cold War: Murphy, Kondrashev, and Bailey, *Battleground Berlin* (see also page 18). His coauthor, Kondrashev, was a retired KGB lieutenant general who, Murphy wrote the author, supervised Soviet counterespionage operations in Berlin from Moscow in 1945 to 1946 as a rst lieutenant.

9. Cable from AB-16 (the author) to Amzon, November 23, 1945, forwarded with letter to the author from David E. Murphy, November 9, 1993.

10. Videotape by Wolff von Gersdorff, 1992, cited by Sylvia Conradt and Kirsten Heckmann-Janz, in *Menschenraub: Das Doppelte Spiel des Juristen Hans Kemritz*, or "Kidnapping Double-Game by Attorney Hans Kemritz," documentary play broadcast by Deutschlandradio, June 14, 2001.

11. Videotape by Wolff von Gersdorff, 1992.

12. Videotape by Wolff von Gersdorff, 1992.

13. Letter to the author from Tom Polgar, onetime head of the CIA in Germany, July 8, 2000.

14. Conradt and Heckmann-Janz, *Menschenraub.*

Chapter 14

1. De Neufville had turned the Tatra over to the author, wryly saying he got it from its former owner, a deceased SS major general, who had no further use for it.

2. The first five drafts of this chapter were written solely from memory. Two CIA historians, after showing keen interest in the Soviet defector episode, were unable to find confirming OSS documents in official CIA files or the National Archives. Three former OSS colleagues of the author in Berlin did not recall the Vladimir defector episode, but might not have been in the city when it occurred; a fourth, Richard Helms, said, "It is entirely credible." Then, in January 1995, the author discovered confirmation of the trip with Vladimir in the form of three

letters he had written in 1945 describing the wild ride from Berlin to Frankfurt and back. For cover they described Vladimir as a German wanted for interrogation.

3. Telephone interview with Thomas Polgar, October 7, 2002.

Chapter 15

1. Author's letter to Amelia Cutler, November 16, 1945.

2. Author's letter to Amelia Cutler, October 14, 945.

3. Letter from Nathaniel H. Batchelder, headmaster of Loomis Institute, Windsor, Connecticut, to Amelia Cutler, January 8, 1945.

4. Letter to the author from David E. Murphy, November 9, 1993. He also wrote in 1955, "we spent time debriefing these unfortunates and trying to recompense them for their difficulties." See Murphy's more detailed account in *Battleground Berlin*, 16–17.

5. David Murphy specifically asked the author about this omission, which he appeared to consider a major flaw in Berlin SSU operations in 1946.

Chapter 16

1. Although SSU did not then know what lay ahead, the Russian attitude clearly foreshadowed the future effort in 1948 to starve Berlin into submission and thereby force the Western occupying forces to abandon the city to Soviet control. That led to the American-British airlift (1948–1949) that fed and fueled Berlin until Stalin backed down.

2. Top-secret report from Saint (X-2), Amzon (American zone), to Saint, Washington, January 25, 1946.

3. Top-secret X-2 report, "Central NKVD Organization and Personalities Identified," April 3, 1946.

4. Top-secret AB-24 message to AB-51, April 22, 1946.

Chapter 17

1. However, the Swiss restricted purchases to what ration cards and a limited amount of Swiss francs would purchase, and the army vacation order threatened court martial if soldiers used "American money, checks, postal money orders or British pounds" (U.S. Army order, March 5, 1946, assigning the author to a leave in Switzerland). As if to atone for these harsh-sounding restrictions, a Swiss Army pamphlet issued to visiting American soldiers said, "Welcome to Switzer-

land: We know what you have done for us and are grateful for the sacrifices you have taken upon yourselves to bring back freedom to the peoples of Europe."

2. A ski patrol in Europe was unusual then. Probably it was arranged because so many American soldiers were novice or rusty skiers. Fifty-two had been injured before the author arrived. Written instructions advised, "[N]o soldier is to go down the Corviglia trail without a ski instructor."

3. TWA (American Airline), *Parisian Weekly Review*, March 1946.

4. In 1992, when writing this book, the author did ask her. She wrote that a friend of her family was the Belgian ambassador to France; he arranged for her to work for a Belgian diplomatic office in Berlin so that she could improve her German (letter to the author from Robertine Lacquet Juteau, November 10, 1992).

5. During the German occupation of France, certain French joined an underground movement called *La Resistance,* which sabotaged the Germans and was especially helpful to the Anglo-American invading armies at the time of the Normandy landing in 1944. Many of the most fearless members of the Resistance were Communists. After the liberation, some joined the French Secret Service, but did not always disclose their Communist leanings.

6. Letter from Gabriel to the author, Christmas 1946.

7. Sprecher, *Inside the Nuremberg Trial,* 1398–99.

Chapter 18

1. Dönitz was also represented by a defense counsel who towered over the others in ability, although observers didn't fully appreciate that then.

2. One unskilled defense attorney foolishly brought the head of a concentration camp as a defense witness, ostensibly to say, "I gassed the prisoners, he did not." His testimony helped the prosecution, which, through cross-examination, established that the defendant was among those responsible for what occurred at the infamous concentration camps ("The Nuremberg Trial," a TV documentary appearing on public television, December 1995).

3. Dönitz received ten years, others twenty years or life in prison, while many, such as Keitel and Kaltenbrunner, were hanged.

4. Timothy Naftali made a sweep of recently declassified secret SSU documents in the National Archives in Washington and found nothing (letter to the author, September 9, 1994). David Murphy, a retired CIA official who served as chief of station in Berlin, searched all cables and reports from Berlin while he was researching his 1997 book, *Battleground Berlin: CIA vs KGB in the Cold War.* He found nothing with Hahn's name. He even looked in the "Romona" file, code for an SSU project, to discover atomic research by other nations (letter of David Murphy to the author, January 3, 1994).

5. *Encycloepaedia Britannica*, 15th ed., 1982, 548.

6. Letter from David Murphy to the author, January 3, 1994.

7. David Murphy, telephone interview with the author, January 6, 2003.

8. Richard Helms had no recollection of the kidnapping project, but said the author's early draft of the aborted Hahn episode was "entirely plausible" (telephone conversation with the author, September 9, 1994.)

9. Tom Polgar noted that years afterward, the CIA formed a "returnee exploitation group" to debrief German scientists returning from the Soviet Union. For a time this group provided the finest American oral source about Soviet nuclear research and production (letter to the author, August 22, 1994).

Chapter 19

1. See letter to the author from David Murphy on November 9, 1993 cited in chapter 15, n. 4.

2. In 1946, "SSU was so poor that getting cars and tires was a continuing challenge. We could only exist with the Army's charity" (letter to the author from Thomas Polgar, August 22, 1994).

3. Letter from Gabriel to the author, February 3, 1947.

Chapter 20

1. SSU report of January 28, 1947, by AB-36 (Polgar), citing Zig-Zag as its source, sent to the author by Tim Naftali, July 5, 1990.

2. Letter to the author from Tom Polgar, February 24, 1994.

3. Author's letter to Gabriel (agent Gambit), October 10, 1946.

4. Troy, *Donovan and the CIA*, 303.

5. Oral report of staff members at Nuremberg to the author, May 1946.

6. Donovan had liberally overspent his government pay during his wartime service and was half a million dollars in debt (Brown, *Last Hero*, 795).

7. Letter to the author from Barbara Güttler, December 28, 1946.

8. Letter to the author from Barbara Güttler, February 15, 1946.

9. Letter to the author from Gabriel, March 6, 1947.

10. Letter to the author from Dana Durand, March 1, 1947.

11. Letter to the author from Thomas Polgar, November 18, 1992.

12. Letter to the author from Robertine Lacquet Juteau, February 5, 1995.

13. Polgar's remarks to the author in an interview in Orlando, Florida, November 11, 1994.

14. Helms and Hood, *A Look over My Shoulder*, 425.

15. Hersh, "The Stovepipe," 77–87.

16. *New York Times*, May 11, 2003, 4–1.

17. *Wall Street Journal*, June 5, 2003, A-4.

Bibliography

Archives

Documents prepared by me or others for the Office of Strategic Services or its successor, the Strategic Services Unit of the War Department, are, if declassified, now filed with the National Archives. Those not yet declassified remain with the Central Intelligence Agency. Historian Timothy Naftali provided me with copies of declassified documents, as cited in the source notes. David Murphy, a retired CIA officer and coauthor of *Battleground Berlin: CIA vs KGB in the Cold War*, provided facts from, or summarized, the few documents not then declassified.

Correspondence

Over 250 detailed letters that I wrote between August 1942 and August 1947 describe nonsecret aspects of my work and present my observations during the war and after. This correspondence provided much of the detail found in this book.

Books and Articles

Ambrose, Stephen E. *Eisenhower: Soldier and President*. New York: Simon and Schuster, 1990.

Andrew, Christopher M. *KGB: The Inside Story of Its Foreign Operations from Lenin to Gorbachev*. New York: Harper Collins, 1990.

Beevor, Anthony. *The Fall of Berlin, 1945*. New York: Viking, 2002.

Brown, Anthony Cave. *The Last Hero: Wild Bill Donovan*. New York: Times Books, 1982.

Casey, William J. *The Secret War against Hitler*. Washington, D.C.: Regency Gateway, 1988.

Christopher, Andrew, and Oleg Gordievsky. *KGB, the Inside Story of Its Foreign Operations from Lenin to Gorbachev.* New York: Harper Collins, 1990.

Colitt, Leslie R. *Spymaster: The Real-Life Karla, His Moles, and the East German Secret Police.* Reading, Mass.: Addison-Wesley, 1995.

Conrad, Sylvia, and Kirsten Heckmann-Janz. "*Menschenraub: Das Doppelte Spiel des Juristen Hans Kemritz,*" a documentary play broadcast on Deutschland Radio, June 21, 2001.

Grose, Peter. *Gentleman Spy: The Life of Allen Dulles.* Boston: Houghton Mifflin, 1994.

Helms, Richard, and William Hood. *A Look over My Shoulder.* New York: Random House, 2003.

Hersh, Seymour M. "The Stovepipe: How Conflicts between the Bush Administration and the Intelligence Community Marred the Reporting on Iraqi Weapons." *New Yorker Magazine* (October 27, 2003): 77.

Hesketh, Roger. *Fortitude: The D-Day Deception Campaign.* Woodstock, N.Y.: Overlook Press, 2000.

Kahn, David. *The Codebreakers: The Story of Secret Writing.* New York: Scribners, 1996.

Keegan, John. *The Second World War.* New York: Viking, 1990.

———. *The Times Atlas of the Second World War.* New York: Harper & Row, 1989.

Masterman, J. C. *The Double-Cross System in the War of 1939 to 1945.* New Haven: Yale University Press, 1972.

Murphy, David, Sergei Kondrashev, and George Bailey. *Battleground Berlin: The CIA vs KGB in the Cold War.* New Haven: Yale University Press, 1997.

Naftali, Timothy. *X-2 and the Apprenticeship of American Counter-Espionage, 1942–44.* Dissertation, Harvard University, 1993. Ann Arbor: UMI Documentation Service, 1994.

Pash, Boris. *The Alsos Mission.* New York: Award House, 1969.

Persico, Joseph E. *Piercing the Reich: The Penetration of Germany by American Secret Agents in World War II.* New York: Viking Press, 1979.

———. *Roosevelt's Secret's War: FDR and World War II Espionage.* New York: Random House, 2001.

Petersen, Neal H. *From Hitler's Doorstep: The Wartime Intelligence Reports of Dulles.* University Park, Pa.: Pennsylvania State University Press, 1996.

Ryan, Cornelius. *The Last Battle.* New York: Simon and Schuster, 1966.

Sprecher, Drexel A. *Inside the Nuremberg Trial.* Lanham, Md.: University Press of America, 1999.

Stiegler, Philip. *London at War, 1939–45.* New York: Alfred Knopf, 1995.

Troy, Thomas F. *Donovan and the CIA: A History of the Establishment of the Central Intelligence Agency.* Langley, Va.: Central Intelligence Agency, Center for the Study of Intelligence, 1981.

Waller, John H. *The Unseen War in Europe: Espionage and Conspiracy in the Second World War.* New York: Random House, 1996.

Warner, Michael. *The Office of Strategic Services: America's First Intelligence Agency.* Washington, D.C.: Public Affairs, Central Intelligence Agency, 2002.

Winks, Robin, W. *Cloak and Gown: Scholars in the Secret War, 1939–61.* New York: William Morrow, 1987.

Index

Note: the letters *pl* following a number indicate the location of a photograph (e.g. a photo of an entry indexed as *4pl* can be found on page 4 of the insert).

About the Author

Richard Cutler is a retired lawyer living in Milwaukee. After graduating from Yale Law School, he worked for Maj. Gen. William Donovan's New York law firm before serving in the U.S. Army Air Forces and the Office of Strategic Services (OSS) in World War II. After the war, he continued to work for the OSS and its successor, the Strategic Services Unit, during the early Cold War. He is the author of *Greater Milwaukee's Growing Pains, 1950–2000: An Insider's View* (2001).